Neural Network Design and the Complexity of Learning

Neural Network Modeling and Connectionism

Jeffrey L. Elman, Editor

Connectionist Modeling and Brain Function: The Developing Interface
Stephen José Hanson and Carl R. Olson, editors

Neural Network Design and the Complexity of Learning
J. Stephen Judd

Neural Network Design and the Complexity of Learning

J. Stephen Judd

A Bradford Book

The MIT Press
Cambridge, Massachusetts
London, England

Second printing, 1991

©1990 Massachusetts Institute of Technology

This book was set in Computer Modern and was printed and bound in the United States of America.

Library of Congress Cataloging-in-Publication Data

Judd, J. Stephen.
    Neural network design and the complexity of learning / J. Stephen Judd.
       p.   cm. -- (Neural network modeling and connectionism)
    "A Bradford book."
    Includes bibliographical references.
    ISBN 0-262-10045-2
    1. Neural computers. 2. Computational complexity. 3. Artificial intelligence.
I. Title. II. Series.
QA76.5.J83   1990   89-13418
006.3--dc20   CIP

Dedication

To Hummeltje Pummeltje, Fin Fan, Mykus Mubbelina, TinkerTankerBelle,
Wiffy Waff, MoLeen, Malaika, Muffin Maid, Teffy Weffy, Hoopey Doop,
Hani, Myka Maybellina, BingabangaBingabangaBingabangaBelle, Lientje,
Marbeleena, Kilko, Munchkins, Tephanie, Mo, Tilkeranasaurus Rex, Lykus,
Finnius Funtubberty, Miss Munkins, M. K. M-J. J-v E., Kiddo, Mousientja,
Rug Bug, Kehwka, FinneFanneFinneFanneFinFan, Hoopey, Dteffy, Myka May,
Phanny, TMJ, Myka Mabel, Tinkerus Tankerus, Muffin, TeffaLieneke, Kgykga,
TinkerBelle, Wiffius Waffientje, Hummeltje, Flintabberty Flonagan, Myka Lyke,
Muffinator, Finnius Fan Tastick, Hum Pum, Lieneke, Mubbeliena, Munkin Maid,
Finne Fannietje, Scoopie Doop, Lyka Mike, Winkerbelle, Fin Fubberty, Babykins,
Winker Wanker Wonderbelle, Marvellyka, Finnius Fumpter, Tilketot, Lyka Tyke,
Tinker Bella Bolletje, Myka Muffin, Monkey Maid, Wiffius Wafoosle, Lievertje,
LykaLeen, Tinker Tanker, Lientje Lien, Mike, Miss Muggins, Scoopie,
Bunby, Myka Mouse, Liffy Laugh, the misses, the Mrs.,
Mahh LYKah, Winkerous,
and all the others
who have
sacrificed
things
in
their
own lives
to accommodate things in mine.

Contents

Contents

Appendices

List of Figures

Series Foreword

The goal of this series, Neural Network Modeling and Connectionism, is to identify and bring to the public the best work in the exciting field of neural network and connectionist modeling. The series includes monographs based on dissertations, extended reports of work by leaders in the field, edited volumes and collections on topics of special interest, major reference works, and undergraduate and graduate-level texts. The field is highly interdisciplinary, and works published in the series will touch on a wide variety of topics ranging from low-level vision to the philosophical foundations of theories of representation.

Jeffrey L. Elman, Editor

Associate Editors:
James Anderson, Brown University
Andrew Barto, University of Massachusetts, Amherst
Gary Dell, University of Illinois
Jerome Feldman, University of California, Berkeley
Stephen Grossberg, Boston University
Stephen Hanson, Princeton University
Geoffrey Hinton, University of Toronto
Michael Jordan, MIT
James McClelland, Carnegie-Mellon University
Domenico Parisi, Instituto di Psicologia del CNR
David Rumelhart, Stanford University
Terrence Sejnowski, The Salk Institute
Paul Smolensky, University of Colorado
Stephen P. Stich, Rutgers University
David Touretzky, Carnegie-Mellon University
David Zipser, University of California, San Diego

Acknowledgments

This book started its existence as a Ph.D. thesis supervised by Professor Andrew G. Barto at the University of Massachusetts, Amherst. His years of patience with my determined excursions into blind alleys were remarkably gentle, supportive, and ultimately productive. The complexity-theoretic content was encouraged, guided, corrected, and made presentable by David A. Mix Barrington. Many useful comments and refinements were made by Ronald L. Rivest.

I thank all my contemporaries in the Adaptive Networks research group at the University of Massachusetts, including Brian Pinette, John Brolio, and especially Richard Sutton, for constant intellectual challenges, encouragement, and resistance; Sara Porat for proofreading my first (tedious) proof; Richard Yee for a conversation about bandwidth and for loaning me a paper on the topic; and Ian Parberry for pointing out the work by Muroga and for determined discussions to ferret out the difference between it and Hong's work.

Thanks go to Tom Boyce, Calvin Jackson, Andy Fyfe, Amy Hendrickson, and Steve Burns for helping me with TeX, LaTeX, MacDraw, an MIT Press macro package, printers, fonts, networks, computers, and other things that are all so easy to use one never needs help with them.

This research was supported by the Air Force Office of Scientific Research through contract AFOSR F33615-83-C-1078 and grant AFOSR-87-0030. The author was also supported by an NSERC Canada Post-Graduate Scholarship. Post-degree revisions of the work were conducted at the California Institute of Technology.

Introduction

Science is taking on a new aspect
which is neither purely physical nor purely biological.
It is becoming the study of organisms.
Biology is the study of larger organisms;
physics is the study of smaller organisms.
—*Alfred North Whitehead*

The puzzle of brain function has endured and fascinated for many centuries. However the fascination has doubled and redoubled in the twentieth century due to the construction of general purpose computers and the subsequent development of profound insights into the nature of computation. Descartes' generation could not imagine a mechanism for thought and intelligence and this inability supported the dualist notion that mental events were quite separate from phyical events. Three centuries have passed. It is now child's play to manipulate ideas in machines, and we have awakened to the universality and ubiquitousness of computation in myriad forms throughout our physical world and in particularly sophisticated and astounding forms in "living" things.

To accompany this explosion of appreciation of the phenomenon of computation, there has been a struggling, straggling effort to prove things about it. What types of things can be computed? And what resources are required to do so? Can we formulate exactly some of the things that brains compute? How must brains be constructed to be able to do the things they do? And how can these imperatives be accommodated in the general supporting technology of tangled masses of squiggley pink and gray nerve cells?

Medical science has tried for many years to understand brain design; one major lesson learned is that the riddles will only be solved through concerted multidisciplinary attacks. In this book I approach the problem using the discipline of computation science and demonstrate how problems in brain science could be attacked from that vantage point.

The study of *neural networks* is one of the new multidisciplinary research fields that has grown up in response to the challenge of understanding the brain, and it is enjoying a large surge of activity. Neural networks are mathematical objects that abstract and distill what we think are the primary computational components in brains. They are being exploited for three broad research purposes:

- as a model of computation,
- as a model of brain structures, and
- as a model of cognitive processes.

This book delves primarily into questions about computation, specifically those computations required to support simple associative memory in neural networks. It is an attempt to understand some of the issues surrounding the phenomenon of learning (or data storage) in networks. Using the lessons learned, it makes some philosophical statements about applying the resulting mathematics to understand and model pieces of the brain. The conclusions should be interesting to anyone intrigued by neural networks, to anyone groping for answers as to how brains are designed, and to anyone following applications of complexity theory.

Many readers who are in the fields of (artificial or biological) neural networks will find the analysis in this book refreshing because it deals with an unusual intermediate level of scale. AI workers, psychologists, and cognitive scientists all treat the brain with a very broad brush and impute structure to it at the highest level. Neuroanatomists deal with real physical structures that have historically been at the level of small organs within the central nervous system. Neurobiologists have been focusing at a very fine level of detail—at individual neurons or even lower down at specific chemical phenomena. The field of neural networks has developed at this very fine scale as well. It specifies a neuron as an abstract function and then asks what small assemblies of such nodes can do.

The study in this book is one level higher than the neuron. It looks at problems arising from having assymptotically large assemblies of neurons. In terms of wet biology, this might correspond to the level of tissue. Remarkably, my results are quite independent of the details in the neurons themselves, and hence a whole set of issues that are relevant at the level of neurons and synapses are suppressed and replaced by a new set of issues at the larger scale. These issues in turn might be supplanted by different ones at the level of small organs.

The issues discovered to be relevant at the level explored in this book surround the allocation of neurons to data; when the network is attempting to store information it must decide where to put what. It must decide what synapses to alter in what ways so as to make an accurate record of the data. This set of decisions turns out to be highly problematic and therein lies my tale.

The inquiry uses complexity-theoretic tools to assess the difficulty of neural network learning problems and to see how the difficulties would scale up for larger networks or for learning larger amounts of data. Readers unfamiliar with these tools of computer science are especially invited to read this book. A secondary motive of mine is to evangelize for computer science and to bring the layman to appreciate how computer science will make crucial contributions to neuroscience. Consequently, I made special efforts to introduce the theory and explain its significance without using excessive formality. The proofs of several theorems are included for those readers who might wish to follow them (or extend them!), but the proofs can also be skipped. Every theorem is accompanied by an interpretation so that nonspecialists can make solid sense of it.

The distant goal of "neural networkers" is to understand how to store, retrieve, and process data in neural networks; ultimately to characterize the types of data that need to be stored, to know how best to represent them, and to see how to design such machines that accomplish it with the greatest engineering ease. I hope this book carries us forward.

Neural Network Design and the Complexity of Learning

Chapter 1

Neural Networks: Hopes, Problems, and Goals

Son of man, can these bones live?
—*Ezekiel 37:3*

... The spirit of the living creatures was in the wheels.
When those moved, these moved;
and when those stood still, these stood still.
—*Ezekiel 1:20,21*

Drawing inspiration from neuroanatomy and spurred on by successes in modeling cognitive phenomena, the *connectionist* model of computation has recently drawn much attention (see the landmark volumes [RM86, MR86, AR88]). We in the twentieth century are not nearly as astounded by wheels and mechanical contraptions as we are by the more ethereal spirits of creatures. We want to know how creatures capture ideas in their brains, how they process information, how they identify patterns, how they store historical data, how they recall patterns and ideas and associate them with new data, how they reason and manipulate abstract concepts. It is because of these fascinations that people have come to study various computational contraptions, including connectionist ones. We hope that by studying devices that are both similar to brains and simpler than brains, we will achieve a more mature understanding of the mind.

Connectionist networks are also called *neural networks*. These networks are used to model how knowledge might be captured, represented, and processed by circuits that are similar in an abstract sense to biological computers. A neural network is characterized by its emphasis on using many richly interconnected processors that perform relatively slow and simple calculations in parallel. The connectionist approach shows promise of eventually providing a new language for designing and building computational devices, and possibly it may yield clues to the centuries-old puzzle of brain function. Many aspects of connectionist networks, including structural design, I/O protocol, and behavioral phenomena, have been compared to biological brains.

The neural network model is loosely defined around three aspects: computing nodes, communication links, and message types. The computing nodes are small, homogeneous, plentiful, simple, and can accept many input connections. These nodes are connected into networks by dedicated low-bandwidth communication links. These links are also considered to be cheap and plentiful—an attitude that is a response to neuroanatomical observations that individual neurons may have extremely high fan-in. The messages sent along the communication links are binary values or perhaps scalar values (e.g., a real number between 0 and 1). One thing we mean when we say the nodes are "simple" is that they react in easily describable ways to their current inputs and do not exhibit much dependence on the recent *sequence* of inputs. (If they could store up and react to an arbitrary sequence of input values, then arbitrary amounts of information would be processable at each node, and it would therefore be trivial to prove that the network as a whole could do fancy types of processing. The trick we want to explain is the existence of *sophisticated* overall network behavior deriving from *unsophisticated* components.)

Given these various constraints, the major domain of design freedom is in the specification of which nodes are connected to which other nodes. As yet, there seem to be few principles or methodologies for designing the specific connectivity patterns in these networks. All network designs in the literature seem to have been rather ad hoc constructions for specific experiments. This is a major inadequacy of the discipline. The discovery of well-grounded and universal design principles would not only assist the development of artificial neural networks but would also strengthen links to neuroanatomy: neuroanatomists might confirm or repudiate the ideas by examining biological brain structure.

Some sources of design constraints arise from consideration of

- memory capacity
- signal integrity (error correction)
- processing integrity (fault tolerance)
- retrieval speed
- signaling capacity (bandwidth)
- 3-dimensional geometry of nodes and links, and the transportation of power and waste heat
- learning issues

A thorough theoretical understanding of these areas would advance the field of artificial neural networks; this book will focus on learning issues.

1.1 Learning

Informally, *learning* is the capacity of a system to absorb information from its environment without requiring some external intelligent agent to "program" it. Learning is a quintessential ability of brains, and it is a major focus of much connectionist research. Unfortunately, the learning algorithms reported in the literature so far are all unacceptably slow in large networks. Although it is clear that we need to be able to scale up our applications to much bigger networks, it is not at all clear how to achieve this. Many researchers view this as the most pressing challenge for current connectionist research.

Neural networks are typically operated in two modes—the so-called "learning" or loading mode wherein data are loaded into the permanent

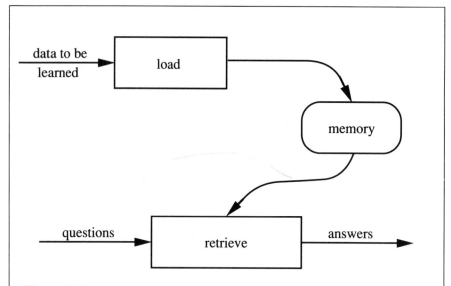

Figure 1.1
A Simple Model of Learning. Note the conceptual separation of the system into two processes (shown in rectangles). This separation does not correspond to any physical separation in a network. Typically, each node serves as a repository for a piece of the memory and participates in both of the processes that interact with that memory.

memory base, and the "retrieval" mode wherein those associative data are recalled from memory. Figure 1.1 depicts the general paradigm. During retrieval, each computing node calculates an output value by some simple rule such as a threshold function on the weighted sum of its current inputs. This simple scalar (or perhaps even binary) value becomes the signal transmitted to other such simple nodes. In spite of the simplicity of the nodes, the network as a whole is expected to do such sophisticated things as associate pairs of bit patterns or find completions of partial patterns.

These comments apply to all types of connectionist models and they also seem to describe standard circuit models of computation. However, connectionist devices are often elaborated with various features like bidirectional connections, learning capability, stochasticity, linear sum functions, or cyclic dynamics. For simplicity, this book discusses only those networks that retrieve data in the manner of a strictly unidirectional feed-forward deterministic circuit. It is assumed that the networks have some means of changing their behavior but that this change does not involve altering their connectivity structure.

An implicit goal of connectionist learning research has been to find a single "learning rule" that each network node can follow in order to adjust the weights used in its linear sum functions in such a way that the retrieval behavior of the whole network eventually implements some desired mapping form inputs to outputs. It was hoped that a learning rule would work for any network design. Many researchers have developed candidates for such a learning algorithm; some notable approaches are the Perceptron [Ros61, MP72], back-propagation [RHW86, Par85, lC85], Boltzmann [AHS85, HS86], and associative reward-penalty (A_{R-P}) [BA85, Bar85] schemes.

There is a theorem proving the effectiveness of the Perceptron for linearly separable tasks in a single layer of trainable nodes. In their book *Perceptrons* [MP72], Minsky and Papert studied this learning rule and investigated several computing properties of 1- and 2-layer networks. But one of the tantalizing gaps that Minsky and Papert left regards the learning problem in *multi*layered networks.

They considered it an important research problem to extend results on learning algorithms for single-layer nets to the case of multilayer nets: "Perhaps some powerful convergence theorem will be discovered, or some profound reason for the failure to produce an interesting "learning theorem" for the multilayered machine will be found." [MP72, page 232]

Descriptions of the back-propagation, Boltzmann, and A_{R-P} methods have each been published along with demonstrations of their ability on *selected* associative learning problems, and their required learning time has been studied empirically (see chapter 3). However, no proof of their effectiveness has been offered and no analytical treatment of their scale-up properties has appeared. The published successes in connectionist learning have been empirical results for very small networks, typically much less than 100 nodes. To fully exploit the expressive power of networks, they need to be scaled up to much bigger sizes, but it is widely acknowledged that as the networks get larger and deeper, the amount of time required for them to load the training data grows prohibitively [HV86, TJ88, Bar82, Omo87]. It is important to find out how to avoid this phenomenon.

The connectionist learning problem is treated here first of all as simple memorization of some given data by a given feed-forward network. This problem is described and discussed in chapter 2. Arising immediately from that is the question as to whether there exists an efficient algorithm for solving this learning problem. "Efficient" is taken by complexity theorists to mean that the worst-case learning time for a network of size n should be bounded above by a polynomial in n. Problems without polynomial-time algorithms are said to be *intractable*.

An algorithm whose running time is always less than $742 + 37.3n^2$ is said to be $O(n^2)$, or "of order n^2". (See page 135 for a technical definition of this notation.) This is a poly-time algorithm, and so is one of order $n^{14.8}$. In fact, the class of polynomial-time algorithms is a extremely generous definition of "efficient" because it allows *any* constant in the exponent; it is quite a strong statement, therefore, to say that a problem is intractable.

That a poly-time algorithm exists for a problem can easily be proved just by exhibiting the algorithm. Proving the nonexistence of an efficient algorithm is not nearly as straightforward (in fact no one has yet succeeded at this), but fortunately an excellent theoretical litmus test is available that is widely accepted as indicating intractability in a problem; and that is to prove the problem to be *NP*-complete. This tool will be explained in chapter 4.

Are there efficient algorithms for learning in large connectionist networks? Or is there some deep reason why there cannot be? Does network design affect learning ability? How does learning time scale up with network size? Can scale-up properties be manipulated through design techniques? This book addresses such questions.

1.2 Approaching the Problems

We seek design principles by appealing to constraints of learnability. As is often the case in theoretical pursuits, it is easiest to investigate extreme cases first, in order to find the boundary conditions where the problem is certifiably easy or certifiably hard, and later to refine the middle ground.

The first step is identifying and formalizing a model of the computational problem involved in getting a network to memorize data. The particular formulation developed is closely related to the types of experiments being reported in the connectionist literature. This formal model is then used to make two important points:

1. The learning (memorization) problem in its general form is too difficult to solve. By proving it to be *NP*-complete, we can claim that large instances of the problem would be wildly impractical to solve. There is no reliable method to configure a given arbitrary network to remember a given arbitrary body of data in a reasonable amount of time.

This result shows that the simple problem of remembering a list of data items (something that is trivial in a classical random access machine) is extremely difficult to perform in some fixed networks.

Of course, connectionists would not be satisfied if all they got out of their systems was rote memory. Much of the fascination of neural networks comes from the possibility of their having generalization properties that could be employed to extend data, smooth over the domain, and induce the structure of the underlying data. Only so would they achieve compact representations, fast calculations, strong prediction, and intelligent learning. We will see that a technical definition of induction as formulated by Valiant can be used to show how the intractability of memorization implies the intractability of generalization as well.

The intractability of memorization suggests that the connectionist model, even though it has demonstrated many attractive qualities, may have a crucial flaw. This might well be a disturbing theorem were it not for other insights that accompany it:

2. There are many ways to circumvent this negative result, and each one corresponds to a particular constraint on the learning problem. There are fast learning algorithms for cases where the network is of a very restricted design, or where the data to be loaded are very simple.

These two observations (the full problem is too hard; some subcases are easy), provide a foundation for theoretical inquiries into the design of connectionist networks. There are various ways to constrain the loading problem to find subcases that are solvable in polynomial time: by restricting the task to be learned, by restricting the architecture of the net, by relaxing the criterion of success, etc., or by combinations of these. The very general hard cases and the very restricted easy cases establish extrema within which a more complete theory can be constructed. This book promotes the usefulness of elaborating such a theory and will consider a few special cases within the great variety of imaginable subcases.

1.3   Subcases

Chapter 5 discusses various ways of formulating subcases or simply different cases that might be feasibly solvable. Even in several of these restricted subcases the intractability remains, thus revealing a labyrinth of open and closed avenues for discovering what it is that large connectionist networks can or cannot learn. What follows here is a description of the major theaters in which constraining conditions can be posed.

Data to Be Learned

By putting strong constraints on what the network is required to learn, some trivial (and uninteresting) learning problems arise. It would be interesting to know if there are some useful classes of learnable tasks. It will be proved that it is intractable for networks to learn even very small numbers of associated pairs or to learn sets of pairs that are drawn from a monotonic function. Both these constraints are so strong as to nearly make a machine useless, so it is discouraging still to find that they are still not sufficient to evade intractability.

Network Design

By putting strong constraints on the type of network used for learning, some trivial learning problems arise. These networks may all be next to useless, but our main theorem shows that when the network is allowed to be of *arbitrary* design, then the learning problem is too hard. The challenge is to see if there are any intermediate network designs that are both useful and easily trainable. Unknown cases include very deep nets and highly connected nets. For various reasons, the study of the loading problem is pursued in one particular broad architectural family called shallow architectures. This family has a technical definition that effectively limits the depth of each network but does not limit the width. This family is interesting because it allows us to study the loading time scale-up issue without having to deal with issues that arise in deep networks. The connectionist literature uniformly reports great difficulties in loading deep nets, so I made a strategic decision to avoid the issue altogether and concentrate on shallow nets. *NP*-completeness appears even in networks of depth 2, so there is still a considerable domain of issues to explore even in the shallow case. Furthermore, the shallow architectures are interesting because they might be a useful model of some brain structures.

For the discussion of shallow architectures, the notion of a support cone is useful. This is just the set of all nodes that can affect the behavior of an output node. To capture how the support cones overlap with each other, a Support Cone Interaction (SCI) graph is constructed. When this SCI graph is a planar, 2-dimensional grid, the loading is still *NP*-complete, but if the SCI graph has limited armwidth, then the architecture can be loaded in polynomial time. Armwidth is a metric on graphs that is a generalization of the more widely known graph-theoretic notion of bandwidth.

Node Functionality

A third way of constraining the learning model is to imbue the network nodes with different amounts of functionality. The standard node type used in connectionist research is the linear sum type—capable of performing any linearly separable binary function. The *NP*-completeness found in our main theorem applies to this case, but this result is refined further to prove that even when the nodes are capable of performing much more complex functions (e.g., arbitrary Boolean functions), or when the nodes are capable of performing only extremely simple functions, the computational problem is much the same. It was hoped that the theory might guide us in selecting appropriate types of nodes, for example by somehow demonstrating that the linearly separable functions are a logical or optimal choice.[1] But the results are quite equivocal on this matter. Subsequent work by Blum and Rivest [BR88] suggests that the linear sum functions actually introduce special computational problems that could be avoided with simpler functions or with more complex functions.

All the complexity results are almost entirely independent of the type of node functions used in the networks. This is a strength in itself. But it offers a further conclusion: that the whole issue of node functionality is of secondary importance to learning complexity, even though significant research effort is now being spent on analyzing the peculiarities of one or two particular favorite types.

1.4   Philosophical Base

This study is based on the belief that the scale-up aspect of the learning issue is a rich source of imperatives for network design and that the development of a theory of learning is therefore well warranted.

---

[1]Recognition goes to I. Aleksander [Ale84] for resolutely avoiding the dominant viewpoint on what constitutes a good node function set, thus prompting my questions on the topic.

The basic position is that a thorough delineation of the polynomial-time solvable cases from the NP-complete cases will illuminate design constraints that all networks must adhere to in order to be capable of learning. Specifically, it is posited that an understanding of the roots of NP-completeness in connectionist learning will yield techniques for building architectures that are easy to load.

Chapter 2

The Loading Problem

An idea is a feat of association.
—*Robert Frost*

Before computer scientists can apply the tools of their trade to a problem, they must first specify very clearly what it is that needs to be computed. They need to know exactly what kinds of data will appear as input and exactly what kinds of data are required as output.

In the first four sections of this chapter, several aspects of the connectionist learning problem are carefully combed into a specification of a computational problem that will hereafter be called "the loading problem." You will find that this formal model is only an approximation to the common connectionist notions of learning, but there are good reasons for some differences. These differences and their justifications are reviewed in the last section of this chapter. All of the prose in this chapter is crucial to understanding the rest of this book; the mathematical notation will be important to those readers wishing to follow the details of later proofs.

2.1 The Learning Protocol

The type of learning investigated here is known as supervised learning. In this paradigm input patterns (called *stimuli*) are presented to a machine paired with their desired output patterns (called *responses*). The object of the learning machine is to remember all the associations

presented during a training phase so that in future tests the machine
will be able to emit the associated response for any given stimulus.
This interaction is diagrammed in figure 2.1.

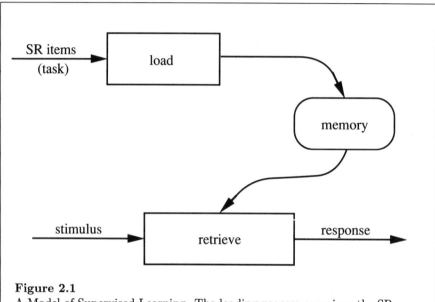

Figure 2.1
A Model of Supervised Learning. The loading process examines the SR
items and alters memory to store that data. Later, the retrieval
process accepts a stimulus and examines memory to find and emit the
associated response.

The exact form of presentation of these data is not of concern here.
Many connectionist experiments involve a long series of training samples wherein a single associative pair is presented to the network at
a time and any particular pair may have to be presented many times
over. But none of these details is relevant here, and our results are
strengthened by abstracting away from them. It is required only that
the associative data are available in some reasonable encoding.

In what follows, every stimulus σ is a fixed-length string of s bits,
and every response ρ is a string of r bits with "don't-cares," that is,
$\sigma \in \{0,1\}^s$ and $\rho \in \{0,1,*\}^r$. The output from a net is an element

of $\{0,1\}^r$. The purpose of a response string is to specify constraints on what a particular output can be: An output string, θ, is said to agree with a response string, ρ, if each bit, θ_i, of the output equals the corresponding bit, ρ_i, of the response whenever $\rho_i \in \{0,1\}$. (Whenever the ρ_i is a "don't care" (i.e., a $*$), then any value for θ_i is acceptable.) The notation for such agreement is $\theta \models \rho$. Each stimulus/response pair, (σ, ρ), is called an SR *item*. A *task* is a set of SR items that the machine is required to learn. To be reasonable, each distinct stimulus in a task should be associated with no more than one distinct response. Equivalently, a task T should be extendible to some function $f : \{0,1\}^s \rightarrow \{0,1\}^r$. Let us view functions as sets of ordered pairs and use the notation $T \subseteq f$ to mean $T \subseteq \{(\sigma, \rho) : f(\sigma) \models \rho\}$. For the less formally inclined, read "$T \subseteq f$" as "the task is correctly performed."

2.2   Network Architecture

The particular style of connectionist machines considered here is that of nonrecurrent, or feed-forward, networks of computing elements. This is a generalized combinational circuit; the connections between nodes form a directed acyclic graph, and the nodes perform some function of their inputs as calculated by previous nodes in the graph.

Define an *architecture* as a 5-tuple $A = (P, V, S, R, E)$ where
P is a set of *posts*,
V is a set of n *nodes*: $V = \{v_1, v_2, \ldots, v_n\} \subseteq P$,
S is a set of s *input posts*: $S = P - V$,
R is a set of r *output posts*: $R \subseteq P$, and
E is a set of directed *edges*: $E \subseteq \{(v_i, v_j) : v_i \in P, \ v_j \in V, \ i < j\}$
The constraints on the edges ensure that no cycles occur in the graph. Denote the *set of input posts* to node v_k as $pre(v_k) = \{v_j : (v_j, v_k) \in E\}$. The size of this set (denoted $|pre(v_k)|$) is called the *fan-in*.

An architecture specifies everything about a circuit except what functions the nodes perform (i.e., what kinds of gates they are).

Figure 2.2 illustrates an architecture with a configuration and a task.

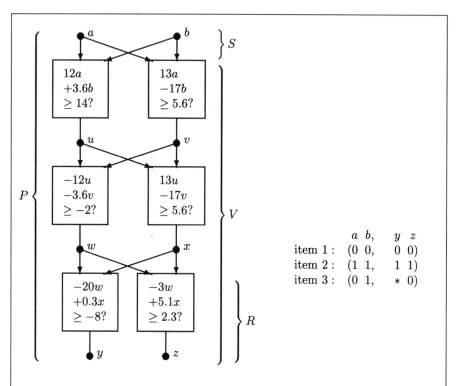

item 1 : (0 0, 0 0)
item 2 : (1 1, 1 1)
item 3 : (0 1, * 0)

Figure 2.2
An example architecture, configuration, and task. The small dark circles are posts; the arrows are the edges (or communication links); together these constitute the architecture. Associated with each non-input post is a square box containing a threshold function; the set of these six functions constitute a configuration. The functions take the value 1 if the linear sum is greater than the threshold and 0 otherwise. For example, when a takes the value 0 and b takes the value 1, u takes the value 0 because $12 \times 0 + 3.6 \times 1 \not\geq 14$. The three items at right constitute a task. Each item supplies values for the a and b posts and corresponding values that posts y and z are required to take on for those inputs. The reader is welcome to work out the output values for each of the three inputs and check that the network performs each item correctly.

2.3   Node Functions

Each node in a network contributes to the overall retrieval computation by computing an output signal as a function of the signals on its input edges. Although most of our theorems can be extended to apply to important types of node functions that yield real-valued outputs, they will be stated and proved just for the case where the functions are binary-valued:

$$f_i : \{0,1\}^{|pre(v_i)|} \to \{0,1\}$$

The function f_i is a member of a given set, $\mathcal{F}$, of functions, called a *node function set*. Typically, connectionists have used the set of linearly separable functions (LSFns) for $\mathcal{F}$. These functions are characterized by a real-valued threshold and a real-valued weight associated with each input to a node. An activation level is calculated from the weighted sum of the a inputs, and the output is one of two values depending on whether the activation is above or below the threshold.

$$\text{LSFns} = \{f : \{0,1\}^a \to \{0,1\} \mid \quad \exists W \in \Re^a, \Theta \in \Re$$
$$\sum_{i=1}^{a} W_i X_i > \Theta \Leftrightarrow f(X) = 1\}$$

Without loss of generality, it can be conceptually simpler to ignore this form of LSFns and think of it as merely a set of binary truth tables.

LSFns as well as a variety of other node function sets are considered. Two of the variants are called AOFns and LUFns. AOFns is the 2-element set {AND,OR} (AOFns is from And-Or Functions). LUFns is the set of all Boolean functions (LU is from Look-Up table). Note the inclusion hierarchy LUFns $\supseteq$ LSFns $\supseteq$ AOFns for any given fan-in.

It is also useful to consider sets of node functions that have real values. Quasi-linear functions (QLFns) are functions composed of any bounded, monotonic function, E, applied to a linear combination of the inputs. (This definition is essentially the same as that used in [RHM86] and [Wil86a].) A special case of QLFns is the logistic-linear functions (LLFns), for which $E(x) = 1/(1 + e^{-x})$. The back-propagation algorithm of [RHW86] is designed to work with LLFns.

A *configuration*, $F = \{f_1, f_2, \ldots, f_n\}$, of a network is a list of n functions corresponding one to one with the set of nodes, V, meaning that f_i is the function that node i computes.

2.4   The Computational Problem

In a configured network, every node performs a particular function and therefore the network as a whole performs a particular function that is a composition of the node functions. An architecture, A, and a configuration, F, together define a mapping from the space of stimuli to the space of responses:

$$\mathcal{M}_F^A : \{0, 1\}^s \to \{0, 1\}^r.$$

The A and F fully define a circuit and thus fully define how the network will behave during retrieval.

A task, as defined above, can be viewed as a collection of constraints on the mapping that a network is allowed to perform. Recall that an SR item in a task is a pair of strings (σ, ρ). When the posts in S are assigned the values of respective elements of σ, the network mapping defines values for each post in R. It is required that these values agree with respective elements of ρ. For stimuli not in the task, any output is acceptable—that is, $\mathcal{M}_F^A$ may be any consistent extension (generalization) of the task.

The process of *loading* can now be defined. In the learning problem being considered, an architecture and a task are given, and loading is the process of assigning an appropriate function to every node in the architecture, $load(A, T) \mapsto F$, so that the derived mapping includes the task. It is a procedure that accepts a pair (A, T) and returns a *solution*, which is a configuration F such that $T \subseteq \mathcal{M}_F^A$. If no such configuration exists, the procedure announces that fact.

The loading problem is a search problem, but it is usual to frame a complexity question in terms of a simple yes/no question usually called

a *decision problem*. In the space of all possible (A, T) pairs, some pairs
will have solution configurations and some will not; that is, for some
pairs the architecture can *perform* the task, and for some it cannot.
The *performability* decision problem is simply, "Can the architecture
perform the task?" In the style of [GJ79], this is phrased as follows:

Instance: An architecture A and a task T.

Question: Is there a configuration F for A
such that $T \subseteq \{(\sigma, \rho) : \mathcal{M}_F^A(\sigma)$ agrees with $\rho\}$?

For purposes of our ensuing complexity questions, this decision problem
embodies the crux of the loading problem, and the terms "loading
problem" and "performability problem" will be almost interchangeable.

Note that the above statements are technically incomplete because
they hold no direct reference to the node function set being used. Our
next (and last) rephrasing of the loading problem redresses this over-
sight and uses classical terminology for expressing decision problems:
The performability problem is the problem of recognizing the following
(parameterized) language:

$$Perf_{\mathcal{F}} = \{(A, T) : \exists F \in \mathcal{F}^n \ni T \subseteq \mathcal{M}_F^A\}.$$

The subscripted parameter indicates the node function set, and in
what follows questions will be asked about a variety of such sets. Each
time the subscript is changed, it will be referring to a slightly different
decision problem.

2.5 Classical Connectionist Learning

The dominant paradigm in current connectionist supervised learning
research follows a style established by the Perceptron many years ago.
The following algorithm illustrates the style using one version of the
Perceptron Learning Rule. Let W be a set of weights and X be an
input vector. Let a be one greater than the fan-in to a node. Then
using a simple trick of notation, the threshold is treated as one of the

weights so it does not explicitly appear in the expression of the linear
threshold function.

```
start:
    choose any arbitrary set of weights W ∈ ℜᵃ
test:
    accept an input X ∈ ℜᵃ
    and a classification c ∈ {0,1}
    if W · X ≥ 0 and c = 1
    or W · X < 0 and c = 0 go to test
adjust:
    if W · X ≥ 0 and c = 0    set W ← W − X
    if W · X < 0 and c = 1    set W ← W + X
    go to test
```

Whenever the weights are adjusted, the retrieval mapping can change.
The process of adjusting the weights is therefore conceptually the same
as choosing a node function $f \in LSFns$.

As exemplified above, the learning process in the classical paradigm
is a cyclic repetition of the following steps:

1. A stimulus is received from the environment.

2. An output is calculated by the retrieval process.

3. Some form of information about the correctness of the output is
   given.

4. A determination is made about how a change in each weight would
   individually affect the overall performance of the network.

5. All the weights are changed according to what step (4) would determine to be an improvement.

The determination in step (5) is made based on information available
locally at the node in question, which in the case of the Perceptron
was only the value of the input relevant to the weight in question and
whether the most recent output was correct. Note that as a conse-

quence each determination regarding a weight is independent of every
other determination, and the amount of information they mutually
have access to is minimal.

In step (3) above, some form of information about the correctness of
the output is given. This can come in various forms, but the most direct
form is simply to be given the correct answer. When such is the case,
the protocol is called *supervised learning.* Variants on this protocol
include *reinforcement learning,* in which the only information given is
a scalar evaluation of how "good" the output from step (2) was. Both
these schemes can be complicated by introducing noise into the data.
In such a case the information supplied in step (3) has only a certain
probability of being correct, so the system is faced with a problem
in stochastic optimization. The literature on learning automata has
studied this extra difficulty in the problem [NT74, NL77, TR81], but I
will resolutely avoid it.

Most connectionist research has attempted to comply with some
present-day notions of neurological plausibility. This tradition is very
much attached to linear sum node functions (primarily LSFns and
LLFns), but the major characteristic of the style has to do with the
way in which the algorithm interacts with the environment and with
its internal state variables. A so-called neural algorithm has a style
substantially akin to the Perceptron's in the following senses: the loading component operates with minimal information beyond what the
retrieval component uses; each node acts independently and somewhat
simultaneously in adjusting its weights; and every node relies on information locally available only, where locality is defined as per connectivity in the net. As is true for the Perceptron, a connectionist
system often has no state variables except its weights, and the meaning of these weights is fully defined by the retrieval algorithm. There is
no significance to these variables beyond what the retrieval algorithm
gives them.

At this time it is difficult to formulate exactly what would be acceptable as "neural," but a loose formal model of this idea would at least
specify a constant number of bits of memory associated with each edge

of the architecture and a constant number of bits associated with each node (both independent of network size).

Any scheme adhering to the general 5-point procedure outline can be treated as an *on-line* algorithm. An on-line system is one that guesses a response to each given stimulus before it is told the required response. Typically the total number of wrong guesses is the sole performance measure of the system. One could view this as a model of an adaptive system having to make tactical decisions in an ongoing environment. Of course, any such system is sure to make *some* mistakes in its guesses; it is interesting to find upper and lower bounds on the number of mistakes an on-line system will make.

2.6   Differences

There are three ways in which the loading problem seems to stray from the more traditional connectionist paradigm. First, there is nothing in our model of learning that reflects any of the neural desiderata. However, this means that any intractability result will therefore be conservative; by deciding not to adhere to these neural constraints the results are strengthened.

Second, connectionists are apt to find the performability problem a strange formulation because from their point of view the architecture is not an *input* to the problem but rather a specification of the machine that is to *solve* the problem. The reason for this formal rearrangement lies in the research strategy of the connectionist community. The prevailing goal has been to find a learning rule that can be employed in each node of a network to pass information back and forth, to witness the various task inputs and errors made during early operation, and to settle eventually on a node function (i.e., a set of weights) that will eliminate output errors. The point to note is that this search for learning rules has historically been a search for a *universal* rule—one that could afford to be oblivious to the type of architecture into which the rule will be deposited to do its work. It has been implicitly hoped that the architecture has little to do with the difficulty of loading. Of course it has always been recognized that the architecture has a great influence over what mappings can be performed, but after assuming that the network was adequate to perform a given task, it was hoped that a general purpose (i.e., non-architecture-specific) learning rule would be able to configure the weights correctly. To accommodate this generality, we must freely vary the architecture when formulating the computational problem faced by such a learning rule; i.e., we must make it an input parameter.

Third, connectionists might again object to this formulation because of the lack of any mention of the architecture in the model of computation that will be used to actually find the configuration. By omitting any reference to the machine, the phraseology above implicitly poses the problem in terms of a Turing machine, or at least in terms of some standard *serial* model of computation. The connectionist approach is to run the learning rule in all nodes of the network simultaneously, so one wonders if this parallel model might not be more powerful. Perhaps so, but note that the number of nodes is at most linear in the problem size (since the input includes a specification of the architecture), so the speed-up due to parallelism can be no more than linear. In the face of the *NP*-completeness result to follow in chapter 4, this is inconsequential.

A comment about the use of the word "loading." The connectionist literature rather uniformly uses the word "learning"; why should another word be used here? First, the word "learning" is used in AI and other fields to refer to a great variety of different things, and it is useful to distinguish some of these uses from others. Second, although the connectionist literature is fairly consistent about what their learning problem is, the loading problem is not exactly the same as that either, so it behooves us to be precise by using a different name for a different problem.

Specifically, the loading problem involves:

1. a given (previously unknown) network,

2. total, easy, ongoing access to the network structure,

3. a given (previously unknown) task, and

4. total, easy, ongoing access to all items in the task,

where "total" means freedom from locality constraints; "easy" means linear cost to read the whole data; and "ongoing" means there is no limit to the number of accesses allowed.

Of the four aspects listed here, (3) is certainly true for the classical connectionist learning, and (1) is often true although implicit. Both (2) and (4) are usually not part of classical connectionist learning. Strangely, although (3) is seemingly paramount, it may be the least important aspect of the model in the sense that knowing the task in advance might not make any difference to the computational complexity of the problem.

Note that (4) implies noise-free supervised learning—the input data are always dependable in that items are always consistent. It also implies knowledge of the exact number of items, something that classical models do not have access to. Aspect (2) indirectly implies that the architecture is fixed and cannot be altered during loading. Both (2) and (4) more or less imply that a Turing machine will be employed to perform the loading function; the algorithm is not required to run on a distributed machine.

The loading problem, then, is a formalization of a particular computational problem that is closely akin to classical connectionist learning but is altered slightly to be on the easy side of three major issues:

- the type of machine used to solve it,
- the style of processing required, and
- the type of information available.

It should be noted that when NP-completeness is found with this model, it is especially potent because it has focused on the easiest and least restrictive conditions for all three of these issues. By applying automatically to many of the more difficult cases, the theory will be comfortably general.

When we find loading to be difficult, we will know that the classical connectionist learning problem must be at least as difficult; when we find loading to be easy, we will have only suggestive evidence that the classical connectionist learning problem is easy.

Mathematics is the predominant science of our time;
its conquests grow daily;
he who does not employ it *for* himself,
will one day find it employed *against* himself.
—*J. F. Herbart*

I don't believe in mathematics.
—*Albert Einstein*

Chapter 3

Other Studies of Learning

A theory has only the alternative of being right or wrong.
A model has a third possibility—it may be right but irrelevant.
—*Manfred Eigen*

Some background in other formal learning theories will help put this work in perspective. It will also help explain why this theory will help connectionist design problems, whereas the others will not. Some experimental results on network learning are also reviewed and all of this motivates the study of the loading problem. However, some readers might find some parts of this chapter parenthetical—indeed the thrust of succeeding chapters can be followed without having carefully read sections 3.1, 3.2, and 3.4.

There is a long tradition of research on the problem of inferring a general rule to describe a set of specific examples. Philosophers [Bac42, Car50], then cyberneticists, cognitive psychologists [HMS66], engineers, and more recently, AI researchers [Mit77, DM81] have all considered the problem. In a distilled form the quest is to find a procedure that can take objects representing positive and negative examples of a concept and find an expression (in some form to be discussed) that describes whether a given object is a positive or negative example of the underlying concept. This type of process is a major component of what is colloquially called "learning." Such inference procedures could be used for classifying unseen examples, for predicting future events, for storing data in a compressed format, or just for storing data in a

convenient format. The last two purposes might be valid even when all
instances of the concept have already been witnessed. My primary motivation is similar to the last one—to store data in a particular format.
More will be said about the first two purposes in chapter 7.

Some mathematical models of learning from examples have recently
been developed. The next four sections will review the relevant aspects
of the learning formalisms defined by Gold and by Valiant and then
contrast these formalisms with the loading problem.

3.1 Gold

Gold [Gol67] established a field of learning theory in 1967 which he
labeled "identification in the limit." He asked whether there is a procedure that could read in an endless sequence of example strings in a
language and eventually find a grammar for the language. See figure
3.1 for a formal definition.

φ is a learning procedure.

t is a text. A text is an enumeration of an r.e. set, which is
   equivalent to strings in a language. Every r.e. set is equal to
   the domain of some function φ_i.

W_i is the domain of φ_i.

t_j is the first j elements of t.

L is a language.

$\mathcal{L}$ is a class of languages.

φ converges on t to $i \iff \begin{cases} \text{(a) } \varphi \text{ is defined on } t. \\ \text{(b) } \exists n \ni \varphi(t_j) = \varphi(t_n) \forall j \geq n. \end{cases}$

φ identifies $t \iff \begin{cases} \text{(a) } \varphi \text{ converges on } t \text{ to some } i. \\ \text{(b) } \mathrm{rng}(t) = W_i. \end{cases}$

φ identifies $L \iff \varphi$ identifies all texts for L.

φ identifies $\mathcal{L} \iff \varphi$ identifies every $L \in \mathcal{L}$.

$\mathcal{L}$ is identifiable $\iff$ some φ identifies $\mathcal{L}$.

Figure 3.1
Gold's definition of learnable (identifiable)

Many other researchers [BB75, Cho80, OSW86, WC80, AS83, Sha81] have built up the theory. The questions concern infinite languages, and therefore they involve infinite "texts", meaning that the system must see unbounded amounts of data. In the main the questions asked place no bounds on time or space required for learning. The flavor is very much like computability theory as opposed to complexity theory.

3.2 Valiant

Valiant [Val84] established a lower-level field of learning, which has subsequently been elaborated by himself and others [Val85, PV86, KLPV87]. His paradigm is concerned not just with what is (absolutely) learnable but with what is *feasibly* learnable (see figure 3.2). The definition of feasibility relies on the well-honored distinction between "polynomial" problems and "super-polynomial" (or NP-hard) problems.

F is a class of programs (concepts).
p is a polynomial.
A is an algorithm.
ϵ, δ are probabilities.
n is a positive integer.
f and g are programs.
D^+ is a probability distribution of positive examples.
D^- is a probability distribution of negative examples.

$$\text{"}F\text{ is learnable"} \iff \begin{cases} (\exists p, A) \text{ such that} \\ (\forall n)(\forall f \in F_n)(\forall D^+, D^-)(\forall \epsilon, \delta > 0) \\ A \text{ halts in time } p(n, size(f), 1/\epsilon, 1/\delta) \\ \text{with output } g \in F_n \text{ that} \\ \text{with probability} \geq 1 - \delta \\ \text{has property } \sum_{g(\vec{x})=0} D^+(\vec{x}) < \epsilon \\ \text{and property } \sum_{g(\vec{x})=1} D^-(\vec{x}) < \epsilon \end{cases}$$

Figure 3.2
Valiant's definition of learnable

Valiant's definition concerns data represented by a fixed (finite) number of variables that typically are all binary-valued. The learning system must discover the underlying rule that describes whether such a given bit string is or is not an example of a "concept." The learner views a series of positive and negative examples of some unknown concept and tries to deduce a description of the concept, so it is similar to Gold's paradigm in this regard, but it is different from Gold's in at least three other regards:

1. fixed-length bit strings, ergo finite bodies of data to purview;
2. bounded time to accomplish the learning, specifically time bounded by a polynomial in various parameters of the problem;
3. specific guidelines as to the form of the concept description.

The third difference is the most fundamental to the formulation and is the most germane to this discussion. Basically, Valiant's theory is intended to determine whether concepts *of a certain class* are easy to learn. For instance, if a concept can be expressed in conjunctive normal form with at most four variables per disjunct, is it possible to deduce that expression from seeing examples alone? If a concept can be expressed as a disjunct of two conjuncts, is it possible to deduce that expression from seeing examples alone?

His definition of learnability has some important other subtleties that capture probabilistic aspects of generalization. These are discussed in chapter 7, but are not relevant to the present purposes.

3.3   The Loading Model

This work describes a third field of learning theory that might be viewed as the lowest level of the three. It is inspired by the computational problem underlying the connectionist approach to learning. Whereas Valiant differed from Gold primarily on the issue of time, Valiant and this work differ primarily on the concern for the circuit involved in representing the data. Our paradigm is concerned not just with what is

$\mathcal{A}$ is a design class of architectures (networks).

A is an architecture (network).

p is a polynomial.

B is an algorithm.

F, G are configurations for A (i.e., settings for all the adjustable variables in all nodes of A).

$\mathcal{M}_F^A$ is the mapping behavior of A when configured with F.

$T \subseteq \{(\sigma, \rho) | \mathcal{M}_F^A(\sigma) = \rho\}$ is a task.

$$\text{``}\mathcal{A}\text{ is loadable''} \Longleftrightarrow \begin{cases} (\exists p, B) \text{ such that} \\ (\forall A \in \mathcal{A})(\forall F \text{ for } A)(\forall T \subseteq \mathcal{M}_F^A) \\ B \text{ halts in time } p(|A| + |T|) \text{ with} \\ \text{output } G \text{ such that } T \subseteq \mathcal{M}_G^A \end{cases}$$

Figure 3.3
My definition of learnable (loadable)

feasibly learnable but with what is feasibly learnable in a machine *with a certain fixed structure*. It shares the same similarities and differences with Gold as Valiant, but its "specific guidelines as to the form" of the representation (item 3) are even more strict than are Valiant's. See figure 3.3. It requires that a representation for the learned data be found that can be embodied in a specific network structure. To achieve it, details of the function at each point in the net are alterable, but no alterations to the connectivity of the network are allowed. For example, if the given network were:

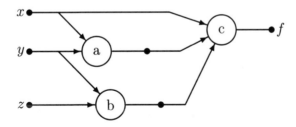

and the data to be learned were given as several specifications of values for the four variables $f, x, y,$ and z, then the objective of the learning system would be not only to discover the function $f(x, y, z)$ but also to find three more functions a, b, and c such that $f(x, y, z) = c(x, a(x, y), b(y, z))$. This is more constrictive than Valiant's formulation because Valiant places only general grammatical guidelines on the form of f where we have an exact expression, minus only the specifications of a, b, and c. This prior knowledge of the form does not make the general learning paradigm any easier or harder, merely different. It asks a question about whether a *particular* network can be made to represent some data, not whether it is possible to to find *some* network to represent those data.

This question is relevant to connectionists because it preserves the more sacrosanct network structure while fiddling the node functions. It is a major tenet of the connectionist attitude that the machine's gross structure (architecture) does not change and that its fine structure (node functions) does. At least to a first approximation this is an indispensable aspect of the connectionist model.

3.4   Comparison Summary

This section summarizes the similarities and differences between the three learning paradigms being considered.

Motivation

Gold's study of comparative grammars is an attempt to characterize the class of natural languages through formal specification of their grammars. His original motivation for setting up a formal learning theory was not to understand learning for its own sake but to develop a tool to understand natural languages. In attempting to define what a natural language is, he looked for constraints on its form provided by the observable fact that two-year-olds can learn it. Furthermore, they learn it mostly by listening to others speak it. Thus this formal learning theory was originally conceived to assist the comparative study of grammars, but it ultimately might contribute to theories of psychology or neural architecture.

Valiant's motivation can be viewed as an attempt to develop a foundation for learning in AI. He wants to discover good models relevant to building devices that can learn and to find the limits to what can be feasibly learned. True to traditions of AI, he uses an abstract Turing machine as the model of computation. Hence his paradigm is not concerned with any structural or functional constraints on the algorithms; it merely requires that an algorithm complete its task within a certain amount of time. Valiant's formulation is exactly relevant to AI, which shares these same freedoms and constraints.

Our motivation arises from the search to understand a very particular computational model. Like Gold, we use it not directly for its own sake but as a tool to constrain an ulterior theory: Desiring to understand neural computation, we seek constraints on network design provided by the computational feasibility of connectionist learning.

Environment

One of Gold's original definitions is of an *informant*, which is a particular kind of "environment" or protocol for interaction between a learning system and a source of data. An informant is an environment in which strings are presented serially to a machine paired with an indication of whether that string is in the target language or not.

Like Gold, Valiant explores a variety of environments, but one environment is quite similar to an informant. His terminology for it is "positive and negative examples" of a concept.

In the loading problem the protocol for gathering information is also quite similar to Gold's informant. The learner's object is to remember what response string is appropriate for each given stimulus string. If the response string were only one bit long, it would be equivalent to saying IN/OUT (à la Gold) or POS/NEG (à la Valiant). The response string is a useful generalization of the one-bit notion but is not a conceptual deviation from the basic idea.

Hence we can consider the three paradigms as having nearly equivalent learning environments. In fact, it is this commonality of supervised learning that makes the comparisons meaningful.

Requirements

In broad terms each formulation is phrased as "For each member of problem class X, and for each of many different ways of presenting the learning data, the class is said to be learnable if there is a dependable way to remember the data." The first two clauses in this sentence correspond to different formalisms in each paradigm:

paradigm	For each member of the class	For each presentation of the data
Gold	$(\forall L \in \mathcal{L})$	$(\forall$ texts for $L)$
Valiant	$(\forall f \in F)$	$(\forall D^+, D^-)$
loading	$(\forall A \in \mathcal{A})$ $(\forall$ configurations F for $A)$ $(\forall T \subseteq \mathcal{M}_F^A)$	$(\forall$ permutations of $T)$

Grammatical Focus

Gold studies the relation between finite evidence and infinite languages. This necessarily involves a grammar, but the form of the grammar is not explicitly mentioned. For example, he asks whether it is possible to find a description (i.e., a grammar) for any given recursively enumerable set.

The other two models can be cast in terms of grammars and languages as well. The data structure resulting from Valiant-type learning can be seen as a "sentence" in a language described by grammatical syntax rules, where neither the words nor their interrelationships are known a priori but where the grammar serves as a validity test for the sentence. Valiant studies the relation between such a grammar for representation and the complexity of finding an appropriate sentence complying with that grammar. For example, he asks how hard it is to find a 3-CNF expression for a given body of data. The grammar involved is "3-CNF-ness", and the sentence sought would have to be a 3-CNF expression.

The loading formalism sets up questions about the relation between a grammar and the complexity of finding words to fill a specific sentence structure from that grammar. The data structure sought is more particular than Valiant's in that it is not *any* sentence from some grammar but is a *particular* sentence from it. For example, I ask how hard it is to load a network drawn from the family of two-layered networks. Two-layered-ness would be the "grammar." The specific "sentence" involved could be the example network used on page 31, and using that example, the "words" sought would be specifications of the functions *a*, *b*, and *c*. The position and relationships of each "word" are fully specified in advance, and the learning system need only discover what the missing words are.

Quantitative comparison

Various quantities involved in the three formulations are compared in this table:

	feature space	input size	output size	time	data structure
Gold	unbounded	infinite	finite	finite	any
Valiant	fixed	bounded	bounded	bounded	constrained
loading	fixed	bounded	fixed	bounded	fixed

3.5   Studies in Connectionist Learning

Many researchers have developed algorithms for supervised learning in connectionist networks. A good review is given by Hinton [Hin87]. Some of the approaches most relevant to our study are the Perceptron [Ros61, MP72], linear associators [And72, Koh77, Koh84] backpropagation [RHW86, Par85, lC85], and the associative reward-penalty (A_{R-P}) scheme [BA85, Bar85]. All of these are "neural" algorithms for feed-forward networks.

A neural algorithm has been given for Boltzmann machines [AHS85, HS86], which is a recurrent network. Hopfield [Hop82] gives a non-neural method, also for training recurrent networks. But such machines have a dynamic retrieval mechanism, and the loading formalism is not relevant to it. For unsupervised learning paradigms, research has been done including [RZ85, and references therein]. The present work does not speak directly to this paradigm either, so none of it will be reviewed here.

Analyses of the feed-forward models have been mostly for a single linear threshold unit or for a 2-layered machine where only one layer is trainable (Perceptron). A *layered* machine is one where the nodes are divided into disjoint sets called layers, network inputs are connected only to the first layer, and subsequent layers get their input signals only from a previous layer. There have also been some investigations of more general structures, which will be reviewed after considering the work on simple networks.

Simple Networks

In the one-layer case, learnability results span a great range. Some problems are impossible to solve; some can be solved "in the limit," i.e., by using infinite time; some have time bounds that are known only to be finite; some have exponential time; some polynomial; and some logarithmic. The scaling arguments are with respect to s, the number of bits in the input vector/string. They are considered here in this same order.

Impossible: There are not nearly as many linearly separable functions as there are general Boolean functions on $\{0,1\}^s$, so most Boolean functions on a large number of variables can not be performed (or perforce, learned) by a single-node linear threshold unit. In their book *Perceptrons: An Introduction to Computational Geometry* [MP72], Minsky and Papert answered questions regarding the functional powers of the 2-layer model and characterized classes of functions that could not be performed when the first layer has bounded fan-in. Of course, any function can be performed with an exponential number of units having unbounded fan-in, but this is clearly impractical.

Infinite: Several asymptotic results have been given for stochastic approximation methods [SW81, DH73], for stochastic learning automata [NT74], and for a combination of these [BA85]. For instance, when placed in a stochastic setting, and modified by gradually reducing the adjustment constant, the classic Widrow-Hoff rule [WH60] has been shown to converge asymptotically to the solution of least squared error with probability 1. Another convergence theorem was given by Barto and Anandan [BA85] for a difficult reinforcement training protocol that involves noisy data and an impoverished form of feedback. They proved in a restricted case that the stochastic A_{R-P} procedure in one node will almost surely converge to correct responses. But these convergence theorems are only for *asymptotic* performance, which means the time upper bound is infinite.

Finite: Rosenblatt [Ros61] and others proved a theorem stating that the various Perceptron learning rules will eventually converge to correct weights if such weights do exist. See Nilsson [Nil65] for notes on the history of its various proofs. This development demonstrated that the Perceptron would learn in finite time, even though it was a very simple and "neural" device.

Exponential: Muroga [Mur65] showed that there are linearly separable functions whose weights are approximately as large as 2^s. Thus even when the function is performable, it will take the various Perceptron learning rules $\Omega(2^s)$ adjustments[1] before getting acceptable weights. Hampson and Volper [HV86] extended the argument to the average case (as opposed to the worst case) and derived a bound of $\Omega(1.4^s)$.

Tesauro [Tes87] measured learning time as a function of the size of the task. He used three networks of a particular style, one particular algorithm (back-propagation), and one particular function from which he draws t random items to make up a task. He then plotted learning

---

[1]The $\Omega()$ and $O()$ notation is explained on page 135.

time as a function of t and found it to be the sum of a polynomial and an exponential. The polynomial dominated in the low ranges but, after a certain point, the exponential dominated.

NP-complete: Peled and Simeone [PS85] proved that it is *NP*-complete to decide if a function given in disjunctive normal form is linearly separable. This problem is more difficult than the loading problem in that it has a very short input and must capture the whole function in a set of weights. The loading problem has a much longer (extensional) representation of the desired function (which by the definitions of complexity affords an algorithm more time to run) and only requires the net to remember those items that are explicitly given. So with less to do and more time to do it, our loading problem is computationally easier; therefore their result is not tight enough for our purposes.

Polynomial: Hampson and Volper [HV86,VH86,HV87] explored several algorithms and learning situations for the single Perceptron to see how they behave as the number of input bits, s, is scaled up. They report exponential times for all but a few simple cases. When the additional input bits are irrelevant or redundant, or when the task being learned is an OR or AND, then algorithms exist with running times that are low polynomials in s.

Logarithmic: Littlestone [Lit87] found polynomial on-line mistake-bounds for a variety of classes of functions. He considered a node function set with the same form as linear threshold functions but demanded a minimum amount of separability between the different classes. (This restriction is a very appealing refinement to the model of a "neural" node function set, since it allows the separating plane to be placed anywhere within a range and thereby relaxes the unrealistic requirement for arbitrary precision in the weights.) For the case where the target function is a simple disjunction of some subset of the input bits, he gave an algorithm that makes $O(k \log s)$ mistakes, k being the size of the relevant subset. When learning k-DNF expressions (for some fixed k), his algorithm has an upper bound of $O(kl \log s)$ mistakes. (l is the length of the expression learned, and s essentially measures the number of irrelevant input bits.) This is remarkable both for being linear in k and for being logarithmic in s.

All these learning results are for single nodes (possibly preceded or followed by a layer of other nonlearning nodes). They shed little light on our question about large, arbitrarily shaped networks.

Complex Networks

Some attempts have been made to analyze the behavior of learning algorithms in the context of composite networks. Rumelhart, Hinton, and Williams [RHW86] have shown that when the generalized delta rule is used in an arbitrary feed-forward network for making weight updates, the net has a gradient-descent behavior. This is a pleasing result but there are at least two deficiencies: (1) no time bounds are available yet, and (2) because the surface in weight space is multimodal, the algorithm may descend into a local minimum and thereby never discover fully correct responses.

Tesauro and Janssens [TJ88] report empirical results studying the relationship between learning time and the predicate order, q, of a task. They measure a series of (network, task) pairs parameterized only by q. The net has q inputs, $2q$ nodes in the first layer (fully connected to each input) and a single output node (fully connected to each node in the first layer). The task is a complete listing of the $t = 2^q$ items for the parity function on q bits. When trained using back-propagation, they observe learning times of approximately 4^q. Since the task has size 2^q, this means the training time is $4^q/2^q = 2^q$ times the amount of data to be learned. This result might also be reinterpreted as evidence that the learning time scaled exponentially in the size of the network.

The Bottom Line

In summary, there is good experimental evidence that training large neural networks is extremely time-consuming, and there is good theoretical evidence that the difficulties are intrinsic. Overall, these various results give one the impression that some very simple over-constrained learning problems are easy, but when the problems are made only slightly more general they become intractable.

However, none of the results are really conclusive for networks of arbitrary shape. Networks of some special designs might find it easy to learn some of those functions that were found difficult to learn in one-node or two-layer designs; conversely, they might find some easy ones hard. We need a more general theory.

Even beyond the specific studies reviewed here, it is widely acknowledged that as networks get larger and deeper, their learning time grows prohibitively. The scale-up issue is therefore an important research problem for current connectionist research.

Chapter 4

The Intractability of Loading

We used to think that if we knew one,
we knew two,
because one and one are two.
We are finding that we must learn
a great deal more about 'and'.
—*Sir Arthur Eddington*

Our major question is about the intrinsic nature of the learning problem
we have posed: How difficult is it to load a given task into a given
architecture? How much time is necessary? As discussed in section
2.4, this amounts to asking how many computing steps are required for
a Turing machine to recognize the following language:

$$Perf_{\mathcal{F}} = \{(A, T) : \exists F \in \mathcal{F}^n \ni T \subseteq \mathcal{M}_F^A\}.$$

(Terminology used here and the related complexity-theoretical concepts
of *NP*-completeness are explained thoroughly in Garey and Johnson
[GJ79].) *NP*-completeness is at present the only good tool we have
for identifying difficult computational problems, but it has a quirky
nature to it in that it is only makes a statement about asymptotic
scale-up behaviour. Technically, this requires that we talk about an
infinite number of different possible instances, and thus about a family
of instances that are without any bound on their size.

The measure of how difficult a decision problem is must be relative to the size of a particular instance of the problem. The size of an instance of the performability problem is taken to be the number of bits that it takes to represent the instance, i.e., the architecture and the task. This number is roughly proportional to $|A| + |T|$. As the architecture gets bigger or as the task gets bigger, one would expect any algorithm to take more time to solve it, but the question we would like to answer is "How much longer?" What is the asymptotically minimum function $g(x)$ for the worst-case amount of time required to solve an instance of size x?

It is proved below that $Perf_{AOFns}$ is NP-complete. This means that it belongs to a class of computational problems for which no polynomial time algorithms have ever been found. All NP-complete problems can be transformed into any other NP-complete problem in polynomial time, so the development of a polytime algorithm for $Perf_{AOFns}$ would automatically give a polytime solution to all of the others. In fact it would make the breathtaking implication that a deterministic machine could solve all the same problems that could be solved by a nondeterministic machine (i.e., a machine with a psychic ability to guess solutions) with no more than a polynomial degradation in running time. Technically, this breakthrough would be expressed as $P=NP$, and it would appear in big headlines in the world's newspapers right beside stories about nonpolluting energy and free lunches for everyone. Although it did appear once in the New York Times, it was quickly retracted as an error and is generally believed to be exceedingly implausible. Indeed, decades of experience have shown that the scale-up function for all known algorithms for any NP-complete problem is an exponential expression whose value is unmanageably large even at small instances of the problem [GJ79, AHU74].

The fact that $Perf_{AOFns}$ is NP-complete is not a statement about the running time for one particular learning algorithm, nor about the idiosyncracies of a particular message-passing scheme, nor about the signalling capacities of simple neurons—it is a result about the intrinsic difficulty of the underlying computational problem. Hence it is not practical to try to decide large instances of the performability question, no matter what method is used. (The instance of a loading problem is large when the network itself is large, even though there might only be a small amount of data to be loaded.) Of course there are some large instances where one can stumble onto a correct decision quickly, but *no* learning rule can *always* solve this problem in polynomial time.

Furthermore, because this decision problem is no harder than the search problem from which it is distilled, the loading problem per se is also intractable. Assuming $P \neq NP$, no general-purpose algorithm can be developed for use in arbitrary architectures that is guaranteed to load any given performable task in polynomial time. (This is true whether the algorithm is conceived as a nodal entity working in a distributed fashion with other nodes, or as a global entity working in a centralized fashion on the network as a whole.)

The parallelism inherent in most neural network systems does not avoid this intractability. An exponential expression (c^x) cannot be contained by dividing it by a linear expression (cx). In many connectionist approaches to learning, there is a strong reason why large numbers of computing elements will not accomplish the loading problem in feasible time: By doubling the number of nodes available, you are doubling the computational resources but you may also be doubling (or even squaring!) the amount of computing that has to be done. Naive attempts to exploit parallelism can actually be counterproductive.

Even with the very best exploitation of parallelism, the running time would still be $1/x$ times an exponential in x and would thus not grant a big increase in the maximum instance size that could be feasibly attacked. Hence it might appear that we cannot hope to build large connectionist networks that will reliably learn simple supervised learning tasks.

The following section states and proves the fundamental theorem for one node function set, and section 4.2 shows how the result also applies to most other node function sets. Readers who wish to follow later proofs in this book should examine this one closely, for all the later ones are based on it.

4.1   Proof of General Case using AOFns

To prove a problem, P_1, to be NP-complete, one must take another problem, P_2, that is known to be NP-complete and transform it into P_1. That is, one must give a polynomial time algorithm that can translate any arbitrary instance of P_2 into an instance of P_1 that is "true" if and only if the instance of P_2 is "true." This algorithm is then called a "reduction from P_2 to P_1" and is formally abbreviated as $P_2 \propto P_1$. See [GJ79] for an explanation of this technique.

Of course if there is a polytime solution to P_1, there will automatically be a polytime solution to P_2 by first applying the reduction algorithm and then the solution algorithm, but since such a composed procedure is presumed not to exist, this technique suffices to convince us there is no polynomial time solution for P_1 either.

The particular NP-complete problem used here in the role of P_2 is called 3SAT. An instance of 3SAT is a expression in Boolean variables given in conjunctive normal form (i.e., a conjunction of disjunctions) in which all the disjunctions have exactly three literals. A literal is a logical variable or its negation. Each disjunction is called a clause. The instance is said to be "true" (or *satisfiable*) if the variables can all be given values such that the whole logical expression is true. For example, the expression $(x_1, x_3, \overline{x_4})(x_2, \overline{x_3}, x_4)(\overline{x_1}, x_2, x_3)$ is satisfied by the assignments $x_1 = 0$, $x_2 = 1$, $x_3 = 1$, $x_4 = 0$. (Assume the usual convention of identifying true with 1 and false with 0.)

THEOREM 1 *Perf$_{AOFns}$* is NP-complete.

Proof: by reduction from 3SAT. Let the 3SAT problem be (Z, C) where Z is a set of variables $\{\zeta_1, \zeta_2, \zeta_3, \ldots\}$ and C is a set of disjunctive clauses over them. Each clause has three literals. For (Z, C) to be satisfiable, there must be an assignment $\Pi : Z \rightarrow \{0, 1\}$ such that at least one literal in each clause has value 1.

A formal construction is given here for the architecture and task, followed by an exposé. Let $w = |Z|$ be the number of variables and $m = |C|$ the number of clauses. The 3SAT instance (Z, C) is reduced

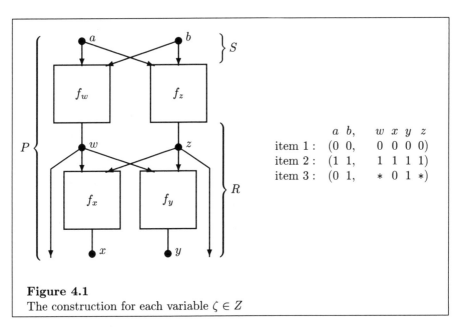

Figure 4.1
The construction for each variable $\zeta \in Z$

to (A, T), an instance of the loading problem, where

$$A = (P, V, S, R, E)$$
$$S = \{a, b\}$$
$$R = V = \{w_i, x_i, y_i, z_i : \zeta_i \in Z\} \cup \{c_j : C_j \in C\}$$
$$P = S \cup V$$
$$E = \{(a, w_i), (a, z_i), (b, w_i), (b, z_i),$$
$$(w_i, x_i), (w_i, y_i), (z_i, x_i), (z_i, y_i) : \zeta_i \in Z\}$$
$$\cup \{(w_i, c_j) : \zeta_i \in C_j\} \cup \{(z_i, c_j) : \overline{\zeta_i} \in C_j\}$$
$$T = \{I_1, I_2, I_3\}$$
$$I_1 = (0\ 0, (0\ 0\ 0\ 0)^w\ 0^m)$$
$$I_2 = (1\ 1, (1\ 1\ 1\ 1)^w\ *^m)$$
$$I_3 = (0\ 1, (*\ 0\ 1\ *)^w\ 1^m)$$

This arcane piece of notation is explained in a two-stage reader-friendly example. Stage 1: For every variable $\zeta_j \in Z$ construct the partial architecture and partial task shown in figure 4.1. From item 1 we know that $f_w(0,0) = f_z(0,0) = 0$; hence $f_x(0,0) = 0$ and $f_y(0,0) = 0$. From item 2 we know that $f_w(1,1) = f_z(1,1) = 1$; hence $f_x(1,1) = 1$ and $f_y(1,1) = 1$. By comparing item 2 and item 3 we know

$$f_x(f_w(1,1), f_z(1,1)) = 1 \neq 0 = f_x(f_w(0,1), f_z(0,1))$$

$$f_w(1,1) \neq f_w(0,1) \text{ or } f_z(1,1) \neq f_z(0,1)$$

$$1 \neq f_w(0,1) \text{ or } 1 \neq f_z(0,1). \tag{4.1}$$

By comparing item 1 and item 3 we know

$$f_y(f_w(0,0), f_z(0,0)) = 0 \neq 1 = f_y(f_w(0,1), f_z(0,1))$$

$$f_w(0,0) \neq f_w(0,1) \text{ or } f_z(0,0) \neq f_z(0,1)$$

$$0 \neq f_w(0,1) \text{ or } 0 \neq f_z(0,1). \tag{4.2}$$

And from (4.1) and (4.2) we conclude $f_w(0,1) \neq f_z(0,1)$. We will associate some SAT variable ζ_j with the group of nodes in this construction. For mnemonic value and brevity, let $\langle \zeta_j \rangle$ stand for "the value computed by the w-node in the block of nodes associated with ζ_j when given the input 0 1". And let $\langle \overline{\zeta_j} \rangle$ stand for its negation, i.e., the output from the z-node for input 0 1.

Stage 2: For each clause in the SAT system construct a single node in the second layer of the architecture with inputs from all nodes associated with its participating literals. Putting variables' nodes and the clause node together, we get what is shown in figure 4.2. It shows the construction for an example SAT system consisting of only one clause $(\zeta_1, \overline{\zeta_2}, \overline{\zeta_3})$. Observe that each item consists of the stimulus from an item from figure 4.1, three replications of its response (one per variable), and another response bit for the clause node (node c).

Claim: The constructed architecture can perform the task iff the SAT instance is satisfiable.

Proof: Remember that $f_w(0,0) = 0$ and $f_z(0,0) = 0$ in each variable construct, so inputs to c are all 0 in item 1. Item 3 has inputs 0 1 so

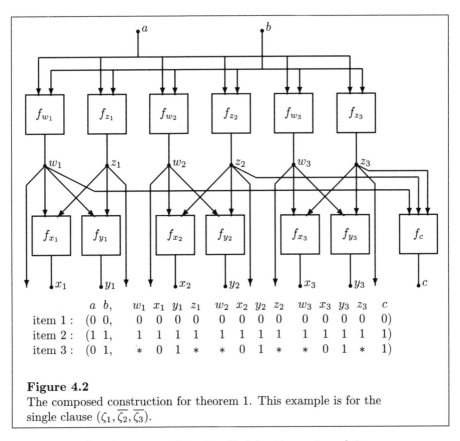

				a	b,		w_1	x_1	y_1	z_1	w_2	x_2	y_2	z_2	w_3	x_3	y_3	z_3	c
item 1 :				(0	0,		0	0	0	0	0	0	0	0	0	0	0	0	0)
item 2 :				(1	1,		1	1	1	1	1	1	1	1	1	1	1	1	1)
item 3 :				(0	1,		*	0	1	*	*	0	1	*	*	0	1	*	1)

Figure 4.2
The composed construction for theorem 1. This example is for the single clause $(\zeta_1, \overline{\zeta_2}, \overline{\zeta_3})$.

we can rewrite the constraints implied by items 1 and 3 as

$$f_c(0,0,0) = 0 \neq 1 = f_c(\langle\zeta_1\rangle, \langle\overline{\zeta_2}\rangle, \langle\overline{\zeta_3}\rangle).$$

Hence

$$\langle\zeta_1\rangle \neq 0 \text{ or } \langle\overline{\zeta_2}\rangle \neq 0 \text{ or } \langle\overline{\zeta_3}\rangle \neq 0,$$

which is exactly the semantics of a disjunctive clause. If Π exists then let $\langle\zeta_j\rangle = \Pi(\zeta_j)$, that is

$$f_w^j = \begin{cases} \text{OR} & \text{if } \Pi(\zeta_j) = 1 \\ \text{AND} & \text{if } \Pi(\zeta_j) = 0 \end{cases} \quad \text{and} \quad f_z^j = \begin{cases} \text{AND} & \text{if } \Pi(\zeta_j) = 1 \\ \text{OR} & \text{if } \Pi(\zeta_j) = 0 \end{cases}$$

For all variables ζ_j let $f_x^j = \text{AND}$ and $f_y^j = \text{OR}$, and for the clause node let $f_c = \text{OR}$. The reader is welcome to check that this configuration performs the task.

Conversely, if a configuration exists, let $\Pi(\zeta_j) = \langle \zeta_j \rangle$, and observe $\zeta_1 = 1$ or $\overline{\zeta_2} = 1$ or $\overline{\zeta_3} = 1$ as required. This proves the claim. $\square$

The extension to multiclause systems should be clear.

Thus we have SAT $\propto$ $Perf_{AOFns}$, and it is easy to see that the algorithm for the transformation runs in polynomial time (in fact linear time and log space).

Finally, although it wasn't mentioned before as a requirement, it must be demonstrated that there is a nondeterministic machine that can decide $Perf_{AOFns}$ in time polynomial in the length of (A, T). Writing down a complete configuration of AOFns takes one bit for each node in A; that the configuration is correct can be checked by evaluating each node function once for each item in T; this takes $O(|V| \times |T|)$ time, under the assumption that it takes constant time to evaluate any single f_i.

This, and SAT $\propto$ $Perf_{AOFns}$ implies $Perf_{AOFns}$ is NP-complete. $\square$

This proof is intended to apply to $Perf_{\mathcal{F}}$ for $\mathcal{F}$ being more than just AOFns. Hence it begins by forcing $f_w(0,0) = 0$ and $f_w(1,1) = 1$. This could have been assumed from the outset since $\text{OR}(0,0) = 0$ and $\text{AND}(1,1) = 1$, but these peculiarities of AOFns were deliberately not exploited in the proof. Regardless of the value for $f_w(0,1)$, one of {AND,OR} will satisfy all the requirements, so the proof is strong enough to apply to AOFns while not being specific to it.

This proof uses the "don't-care" symbol, but such is not always a part of the learning protocol used in connectionist studies. In appendix C there is another version of the proof that avoids the "don't-care" by using some extra signals and nodes. I believe this detail does not significantly alter the nature of the problem. The "don't care" is employed in all the other proofs because it removes clutter and allows more transparent constructions.

4.2 Other Node Function Sets

The intent of this section is to demonstrate that the intractability of the performability problem does not depend much on the particular node function set being used—its difficulty remains for essentially all nontrivial cases.

Theorem 1 deals only with AOFns, but connectionist studies typically use LSFns, the linearly separable functions. LSFns includes all of AOFns and, when the number of inputs to a node is large, it is considerably more powerful. It might seem, therefore, that this extra power would make loading easier. Unfortunately, this case (and even LUFns) is just as hard.

COROLLARY 2 For any node function set $\mathcal{F}$ such that all members of F are binary-valued, and $\mathcal{F} \supseteq \{\text{AND, OR}\}$, $Perf_{\mathcal{F}}$ is NP-hard.

Proof: Both directions of the proof of the claim in theorem 1 require nodes able, at least, to perform functions from AOFns. The reduction thus follows for any node function set that includes them. $\square$

COROLLARY 3 $Perf_{LSFns}$ is NP-complete.

Proof: NP-hardness follows from corollary 2, so it need only be shown that $Perf_{LSFns}$ is in NP. For this to be true, there must exist some polytime way of guessing a function from LSFns and being sure that indeed it *is* from LSFns. If fan-in were bounded in our model, then this would be easy since a nondeterministic selection could be made from a fixed table of all LSFns up to that input size. Without bounds on fan-in, though, the table would not be finite and hence this technique will not work. One might attempt to achieve a selection from LSFns by simply writing down the weights that are used in the linear sum, but since the weights are assumed to be *real* (i.e., of a potentially infinite number of decimal places), this technique is also inadequate. However, Hong [Hon87] has recently proved that approximations to the weights are sufficient to encode any and all members of LSFns. Specifically, only a polynomial number of digits are required (polynomial in the fan-in), and hence $Perf_{LSFns}$ is NP-complete.   □

Muroga [Mur71, thm 9.3.2.1] implicitly proves the same result about polynomial bounds on the weights in LSFns. It is tighter but less direct.

COROLLARY 4 $Perf_{LUFns}$ is NP-complete.

Proof: Again, NP-hardness follows from corollary 2, but a proof that $Perf_{LUFns}$ is in NP must give some format for guessing members of LUFns. There must be some polytime way of writing down an arbitrary function and checking that it is in LUFns.

To fully specify an arbitrary member of LUFns requires $2^{|pre(v_i)|}$ bits, and hence it takes exponential time to write it down. (The statement of the theorem implies no bound on the fan-in to a node.) However, each node function will be invoked exactly $t = |T|$ times in the performance of the task; hence one can specify a function $F \in$ LUFns by asserting a default value (1, say) to cover most inputs and then listing the exceptional inputs, α, for which $F(\alpha) = 0$ (of which there are at most t). Since T has a unary encoding of t, there is a representation of F that is polynomial in the length of (A, T), and this means that a function can always be written down in polytime.

Making sure that such a function is a member of LUFns is trivial, since *all* binary-valued functions are members. Hence $Perf_{\mathcal{F}} \in$ NP even when $\mathcal{F} =$ LUFns, and $Perf_{LUFns}$ is NP-complete.   □

LSFns is a special case of the quasi-linear functions (QLFns). Theorem 3 pertains only to discrete, binary-valued signals and does not apply to real-valued quasi-linear functions. However, another theorem pertains specifically to the popular logistic-linear functions (LLFns) used in back-propagation:

THEOREM 5 $Perf_{LLFns}$ is NP-complete.   □

Proof in appendix B. As a corollary, performability with the more general class of quasi-linear functions, $Perf_{QLFns}$ is also NP-hard.

These theorems indicate that the difficulty in the loading problem has very little to do with the choice of node function sets. This observation is strengthened below in theorem 12, section 5.2, which states that some tasks that are performable using very restricted node function sets are difficult to load even when that node function set is greatly expanded. This argues that the difficulties of loading will not be overcome by searching for ever more powerful node types.

4.3 Recap of the Main Result

This chapter concludes with a more convenient statement of the main result:

COROLLARY 6 Loading is *NP*-complete.

Proof: The decision problem is *NP*-complete, and since being able to solve the search problem would allow one to answer the decision problem, the search problem must be at least as hard. □

Note that no node function set is explicitly mentioned in this corollary. There are two ways in which this makes the corollary technically loose. First is that for an absurdly simple node function set (e.g., where the set has only one member), the problem is not *NP*-hard. Second is that deciding membership in an absurdly complicated node function set (e.g., where the truth-table representation of each function must name a halting program) might not be *NP*-easy. However, in the common cases, and in other reasonable cases that have been explored, the result is robustly true. Because it holds for any node function set of interest, specification of the set will hereafter be omitted in order to imply generality.

It is noteworthy that a different proof of the *NP*-completeness of $Perf_{LSFns}$ has recently been found by Blum and Rivest [BR88]. Their proof differs from ours in that different parameters are scaled up. Our proof scales up the size of the architecture and the number of bits in the response strings while keeping the number of items and the number of bits in the stimulus strings constant. Their proof keeps the size of the architecture and the number of bits in the response strings constant while scaling up the number of items and the number of bits in each stimulus string.

It might also be noted that there are node function sets for which performability can be proved *NP*-complete without scaling up the size of the task or the length of the strings at all; using such a node function set, machines of arbitrary size would be unable to load even a *fixed* amount of data!

The sum of these investigations thus far has been to demonstrate that *memorizing associative data is trivial on a Turing machine or a random access machine but it is problematic on a neural network*. Harking back to the discussion of learning theories in chapter 3, the distinction that makes the difference here is that the Gold style of question uses the general purpose models (Turing machines and random access machines) to avoid mentioning constraints about the style of representation that the information must be stored in, whereas the questions posed by the neural network model are explicit about many aspects of the representation.

Chapter 5

Subcases

The outcome of any serious research can only be
to make two questions grow where only one grew before.
—*Thorsten Veblen*

Our results heretofore preclude only the broadest, most ambitious interpretation of the goal of connectionist learning. Essentially, the goal that has been formulated is to find an algorithm that is *guaranteed* to load *any* performable task in *any* conceivable net. Theorem 6 implies that this is too hard to achieve. But one can imagine several ways to constrain the problem in such a way that some special regularity in it might facilitate its solution. Such constraints would involve restrictions on architectural design, restrictions on tasks restrictions, and/or different criteria of success. For most such subcases, our theorem says nothing.

This section discusses several ways to define subproblems and/or different problems that may be easier to solve than the general loading problem. Interspersed among these comments are several corollaries to the above proof that state further negative results.

Recall that *NP*-completeness is a statement about an infinite class of different instances of a problem. Hence all the subcases that can be explored must have something about them that scales up to *any* *size*. For example, when an architectural family is defined, it must be an infinite family—there can be no restriction like "networks of fewer than 400 weights", or "all architectures whose size is exactly that of a dolphin brain", for these admit degenerate questions whose answer is not illuminating. Any finite family has a trivial loading algorithm that just consults a table of answers for all the different cases, and we have to avoid this triviality somehow. At this time, the only known mathematical contraption for forcing an algorithm to be doing something interesting is to require it to deal with an *infinite* number of cases.

5.1 Architectural Constraints

First, theorem 1 is a statement about networks and tasks *in general*, but there may be large useful classes of networks (defined by some design restrictions) where loading a task would always be achievable in polynomial time. It has been an empirical observation that although some algorithms (notably back-propagation) work well in nets that have only a few levels intervening between input posts and output posts, they work much more slowly in deep nets. One might be tempted to infer that shallow nets would be intrinsically easier to load. By examining the construction in the above proof, we see this is not so. The construction uses only two layers and yet an algorithm for loading it was shown to be equivalent to an algorithm for solving 3SAT. Hence:

COROLLARY 7 Loading is *NP*-complete, even when the architectures are restricted to be of depth ≤ 2 and of fan-in ≤ 3.   □

Rather than limit the *maximum* depth or fan-in, what is more likely to help is a restriction that sets a *minimum* depth (say as a function of the width of the net), or a *minimum* fan-in, because this forces a minimum number of degrees of freedom everywhere. Since experimental evidence seems to contradict both these suggestions, it would be important to resolve the issue.

Other architectural design constraints have been explored. As a first piece of analysis, we have examined some issues in shallow networks that have gross structure extending through their width. The results are substantial enough to warrant a separate chapter (chapter 6).

One avenue of freedom usually not exploited by connectionist learning schemes is to alter the architecture as learning proceeds. When
carried to extremes, this would amount to an exercise in arbitrary circuit design, rather than in connectionist learning, but adhering rigidly
to the starting architecture may be just too constrictive; somewhere
between these two extremes there may be a balance that combines the
best of both worlds. Valiant and others [Val84, KLPV87] have ini-
tiated the study of what can be feasibly learned using total freedom
of connectivity within a certain class of architectures. For example,
their μ-expressions are the same as tree-shaped architectures that use
AOFns.

It is conceivable that the difficulties in loading stem specifically from
the nonrecurrence of the nets and the fact that all their "knowledge"
about a stimulus must be elicited in one single evaluation of each node
function. If so, then a more reasonable model of network memory
might involve storing data as cycles in state-space where the power of
attractor dynamics could be exploited to make loading easier (albeit at
the cost of more expensive retrieval). Such would be a large departure
from our model, but there are plenty of pitfalls there too; Porat [Por87]
proves that in such a system the problem of deciding just if a configured
network stabilizes or cycles is NP-hard. See also [God87, Lip87].

5.2 Task Constraints

Next, the formulation of the learning problem may be inappropriate
in that it requires a network to be able to load too large a class of
tasks. By using performability as the decision problem, we are in effect
defining the task class in terms of the architecture itself and asking that
any architecture A be able to load any task in its set of performable
ones, $P^A = \{T : \exists F \ni \mathcal{M}_F^A \supseteq T\}$. But it is not necessary to expect an
architecture to be able to load all of these tasks. From a practical point
of view, all that is necessary is that it be able to perform and load some
useful target class, $\mathcal{T}$, of tasks. Obviously, it is necessary that $\mathcal{T} \subseteq P^A$,
and the results herein show that it is too ambitious to have $\mathcal{T} = P^A$

for arbitrary A. However, there are many ways to define $\mathcal{T}$ so as to exclude some tasks in P^A, thus possibly leading to a loadable class. It would be useful to be able to characterize just what target classes of tasks a network could learn or, conversely, to be able to determine what types of architectures could learn a given target class of tasks.

Our main theorem has implications for the restricted classes of monotonic tasks, small tasks, and tasks that are performable using very small and simple node function sets.

Define $\sigma \succeq \delta$ to mean that every element of the binary vector σ is a 1 if its corresponding element in binary vector δ is a 1. A *monotonic function* is a function g such that

$$\sigma \succeq \delta \Rightarrow g(\sigma) \succeq g(\delta).$$

A *monotonic task*, T, is a set of items such that for some monotonic function g, T agrees with g:

$$(\sigma, \rho) \in T \Rightarrow \rho \text{ agrees with } g(\rho).$$

COROLLARY 8 Loading is *NP*-complete even when tasks are restricted to be monotonic.   □

COROLLARY 9 Loading is *NP*-complete even when there are only two bits in the stimulus strings ($s = |S| = 2$).   □

COROLLARY 10 Loading is *NP*-complete even when tasks are restricted to be of no more than three items.   □

These three corollaries give techniques for narrowing the target classes of tasks, but all of them have dead-ended in *NP*-completeness. A more promising avenue is to define the task restrictions in terms of what is performable by a network that is in some way less powerful than the network being loaded. This device parallels the technique used by Pitt and Valiant in [PV86, definition 1.2]. Let us use a *target-net* to define the set of tasks that a *learner* will be required to load. For example, suppose we have a network, A, that can perform a task, T, using only those node functions in the set $\mathcal{G}$. And suppose that another network of the same architecture but capable of using a (larger) node function set $\mathcal{F}$ is charged with loading T. The first network is the target-net and the second the learner. If $\mathcal{G} \subset \mathcal{F}$, then the tasks performable by the target-net will be a subset of the tasks performable by the learner. Is it easier to decide performability of this smaller set of tasks?

To denote this new question, the parameters for describing the target-net are subscripted to the left of $Perf$ and those for the learner are subscripted to the right; the current example is denoted by $_\mathcal{G}Perf_\mathcal{F}$. Formally, it requires for all architectures, A, and for all tasks, T, to be able to compute an output, d, such that

$$d = 1 \;\; \Rightarrow \;\; \exists F \in \mathcal{F}^n : T \subseteq \mathcal{M}_F^A$$
$$d = 0 \;\; \Rightarrow \;\; \nexists G \in \mathcal{G}^n : T \subseteq \mathcal{M}_G^A$$

Note that in some cases $either$ answer would be correct, and hence this is a relaxed form of decision problem.

The question $_\mathcal{F}Perf_\mathcal{F}$ is exactly the original type of question $Perf_\mathcal{F}$.

With this new notation we can strengthen some earlier theorems regarding node function sets. Recall that in section 4.2 theorems dealt with performability problems that were specific to certain node function sets; we investigated how the loading problem might be easier if more powerful node function sets were used. Unfortunately, as we gave the machines more power, we were also asking them to do more; so our theorems were not being played on a level playing field.

The performability problem $Perf_\mathcal{F}$ asks whether a given task is in a certain set of tasks, namely, the set of all tasks performable by a given network. In expanding $\mathcal{F}$, we were explicitly expanding the functionality of the machine but simultaneously implicitly expanding the set of tasks that we wanted to identify. So regardless of the complexity of the new problem, one could not conclude from the theorems whether the extra power was really helping or not. If you want to know if a larger sail will get your boat around the course quicker, you can beef up the sail and find out. But if the wind changes strength before you make your test run, you might not be able to tell anything.

Somehow we have to keep the set of tasks constant while we beef up the node functions. The following corollary will do just that, thereby showing that no general advantage can be made of extra node function power to load tasks:

COROLLARY 11 $_{\mathcal{G}}Perf_{\mathcal{F}}$ is *NP*-complete for $\mathcal{F}$ and $\mathcal{G}$ being any reasonable superset of AOFns.

Proof: This follows by the same argument used for corollary 2. Both directions of the proof of the claim on page 46 in theorem 1 only require nodes able, at least, to perform functions from AOFns. As long as $\mathcal{F}$ includes AOFns, one direction of the proof holds, and as long as $\mathcal{G}$ includes AOFns, the other direction of the proof holds.   □

Just to emphasize how a large difference in node functionality makes no difference in loading complexity, witness an extreme case of the above corollary:

COROLLARY 12 Loading an arbitrary architecture, A, using LUFns is *NP*-complete even when the tasks are restricted to be performable by A using AOFns.   □

This corollary deals with a type of task restriction, but it also provides further evidence that the *NP*-completeness of the loading problem does not derive from difficulties inherent in the node function set. Devising ever more powerful node functionality will not overcome the intractability here.

5.3   Relaxed Criteria

Finally, our mathematical question has a very exacting criterion of success in training: either the machine performs perfectly or it doesn't.

If the criterion was more lenient then the problem might be much easier. Some probabilistic or approximate criterion of learning might be more appropriate. Here is one that won't help:

COROLLARY 13 Loading is *NP*-complete even when only 67% of the items are required to be retrieved correctly.

Proof: Loading slightly more than two thirds of three items is the same requirement as loading all three items.   □

5.4 Summary

Note that all the restrictions mentioned in this section actually hold simultaneously.

COROLLARY 14 Loading is *NP*-complete even when

- the architectures are restricted to be of depth ≤ 2 and of fan-in ≤ 3,
- tasks are restricted to be monotonic,
- there are there are only two bits in the stimulus strings ($s = |S| = 2$),
- tasks are restricted to be of no more than three items,
- only 67 percent of the items are required to be retrieved correctly, and
- tasks are restricted to be performable by AOFns, although a configuration may draw node functions from LUFns.   □

Chapter 6

Shallow Architectures

Without mathematics one cannot fathom the
    depths of philosophy;
Without philosophy one cannot fathom the
    depths of mathematics;
Without the two one cannot fathom anything.

—Bordas-Demoulins

The loading problem is *NP*-complete even for networks of depth two, so rather than attempting to deal with deep nets, we shall limit our attention to shallow nets and try to identify additional constraints that yield tractable loading problems. The following quote by Baldi and Venkatesh [BV87] provides further justification of this strategy:

It is not unusual to hear discussions about the tradeoffs between the depth and width of a circuit. We believe that one of the main contributions of complexity analysis is to show that this tradeoff is in some sense minimal and that in fact there exists a very strong bias in favour of shallow (i.e., constant depth) circuits. There are multiple reasons for this. In general, for a fixed size, the number of different functions computable by a circuit of small depth exceeds the number of those computable by a deeper circuit. That is, if one had no prior knowledge regarding the function to be computed and was given m hidden units then the optimal strategy would be to choose a circuit of depth two with the m units in a single layer. In addition, if we view computations as propagating in a feed-forward mode from the inputs to the output unit, then shallow circuits compute faster. And the deeper a circuit, the more difficult become the issues of time delays, synchronization, and precision on the computations. Finally, it should be noticed that given overall responses of a few hundred milliseconds and given the known time scales for synaptic integration, biological circuitry must be shallow, at least within a "module" and this is corroborated by anatomical data.

This chapter first introduces the notion of a support cone, which is the set of nodes that can affect the behavior of an output node. On this is built the notion of the Support Cone Interaction (SCI) graph of an architecture, which isolates computationally salient features of an architecture by explicitly denoting only the overlaps between support cones. Finally, by applying a limit to the size of the support cones, a type of formal constraint is created that is powerful enough to mask off the difficult issues involved in loading deep nets without interfering with our theoretical investigation into issues of width. The term "shallow networks" will be used to mean a family of networks whose maximum support cone size is limited by some parameter but there is no limit on the number of nodes. This has the effect of defining a family of bounded depth and unbounded width.

It is shown that limiting the size of the support cones is not enough in itself to make loading tractable. Indeed, even when attention is further restricted to architectures whose SCI graphs are regular planar grids, the problem is NP-complete. Only when additional constraints are added that serve to prohibit the existence of large grids within the SCI graph are feasible problems identified: polynomial-time loadable architectures are found for the case where the SCI graph is of limited armwidth.

6.1 Definitions

Definition In an architecture $A = (P, V, S, R, E)$, each output node $x \in R$ has a *support cone*, $sc(x)$, which is the set of all nodes in V that can potentially affect the output of that node; that is, it is the set of predecessor nodes:

$$sc(x) = \{x\} \cup \{sc(y) : y \in pre(x) \cap V\}.$$

Figure 6.1 illustrates this simple idea. The network retrieval behavior at any particular output node is determined by (and only by) the functions assigned to each node in its support cone.

Definition A *support cone interaction graph* (SCI graph) for an architecture is an accounting of the interactions between support cones. It is a graph with nodes $\{z_1, z_2, \ldots, z_r\}$ corresponding one-to-one with the output nodes, R, and having edges $\{(z_i, z_j) : sc(R_i) \cap sc(R_j) \neq \emptyset\}$. In figure 6.1, there are five output nodes (arranged along the bottom) and the support cone for any one of them intersects the support cone for all the others. Hence the SCI graph would be the complete graph on five nodes. Another, more structured, example of a SCI graph appears in figure 6.10.

Definition A *partial configuration* for node x is an assignment of functions to each node in its support cone:

$$F_x : sc(x) \to \mathcal{F}.$$

Figure 6.1 illustrates this idea by naming node functions only for those nodes in one of the support cones.

A *partial configuration for a group of nodes*, X, is an assignment of functions to all nodes in all of its support cones:

$$F_X : \bigcup_{x \in X} sc(x) \to \mathcal{F}.$$

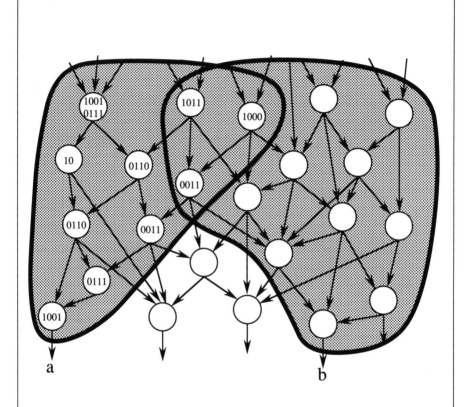

Figure 6.1

Illustration of support cones. The shaded and outlined area
surrounding output node a encompasses all the nodes in its support
cone. Likewise the support cone for output b is shaded in.

Note that the two cones overlap in three nodes; because of this there
would be an edge in the SCI graph between the node for a and the
node for b.

The binary numbers name node functions and as a group they
constitute a partial configuration for output node a.

Definition   The *support cone configuration space* (*sccs*) for output node x is the set of all partial configurations for the support cone of x. If we assume that $\mathcal{F} = \mathrm{LUFns}$, then the number of functions in $\mathcal{F}$ is $2^{\text{fan-in}}$. The binary numbers in figure 6.1 can represent a straightforward encoding of a function from LUFns. The configuration space for node a would be all the possible settings of all these bits, and there are $2^3 \times 2^2 \times 2^2 \times 2^1 \times 2^2 \times 2^2 \times 2^2 \times 2^2 \times 2^2 \times 2^2 = 2^{20}$ such settings. The size of the *sccs* for node b is 2^{33}.

Since we are considering only binary functions of binary values for each node in a finite graph, the size of a *sccs* is always finite.

Definition   A family of architectures is *shallow* if the size of the largest *sccs* in each architecture is bounded. (At first, assume it is bounded by a constant; this will be loosened later.)

Note that this limitation has the effect of bounding the depth of a network, the maximum fan-in to any node, and the number of different functions in the node function set, although it does not dictate how these things are traded off against each other.

The complete *sccs* for any node in any architecture in a shallow family can be exhaustively searched in constant time.

6.2   Grids and Planar Cases

This section starts from our previous *NP*-completeness result on shallow architectures and tightens it to apply to two progressively more constrained families of shallow architectures.

The proofs are extensions of the one used for theorem 1, so we import the construction used there and make a minor change. Note that the construction in figure 6.2a is almost identical to the one given earlier in figure 4.1 (page 45) except that $S = \{a, b, d, e\}$ instead of just $\{a, b\}$. The tasks remain functionally the same, however, because input a is identical to input d, and b is identical to input e.

To make the next proofs easy to read, a pictorial notation for architectures and tasks eliminates excessive formality. In figure 6.2a the

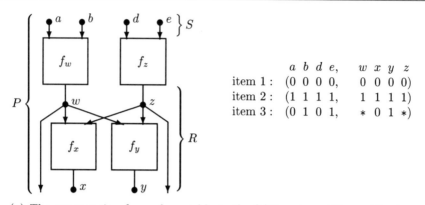

(a) The construction for each variable in the SAT system. The architecture is shown on the left drawn in the classic side view, the three items in the task are shown on the right. Zeroes and ones are desired responses; the asterisks are "don't cares." This construction is nearly identical to the one used in figure 4.1, except that $s = |S| = 4$ rather than 2.

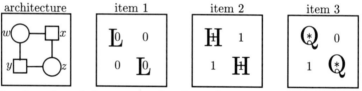

(b) The plan view of the construction for each variable in the SAT system. This is a different representation of what is shown in part (a) above. On the left is the plan view of the architecture. Round nodes are first-layer nodes and each has two external input connections (which are not shown). Square nodes are second-layer nodes and have input connections from the round nodes. All nodes have external output connections (which are not shown). The three diagrams on the right are pictorial representations for the same three items as appear in (a) above. The letter L stands for the 2-bit input 0 0, H stands for 1 1, and Q stands for 0 1. The zeroes and ones are desired responses; the asterisks are "don't cares." Each character is positioned to correspond to a node as drawn in the left diagram. First layer nodes have stimulus bits and required responses as well.

Figure 6.2
Plan view notation

network has been depicted on the page so that information flows across the plane of the page, as is customary in the connectionist literature. Figure 6.2b shows an alternate view of this same architecture, the *plan view*, which is a view "from above." If a network is drawn in such a way that during retrieval the Stimulus originates above the page, information flows into the page, and the Response arrives below the page, then the network is drawn in plan view. The items shown in figures 6.2a and 6.2b are also different representations of the same task.

As in the proof for theorem 1, each clause in the 3SAT system corresponds to a single node in the second layer of the constructed architecture with inputs from all nodes associated with its participating literals. Putting all the variables' nodes together with the clause node yields something like what is shown in figure 6.3. It is a plan-view re-representation of figure 4.2.

As before, the largest support cone in this construction has only four nodes in it and the largest fan-in is only three, so the largest *sccs* is of limited size. Hence this family of constructions fits the definition of shallow networks, and this construction is therefore sufficient to prove what is actually a looser version of corollary 7:

COROLLARY 15 Loading shallow architectures is *NP*-complete. □

After discovering this theorem, intuition might have it that the problem is difficult because the architecture lacks any regularity in its structure—choices for a node function in one part of the network can immediately impact options in any other part of the network. Connections in the architecture can reach and thereby propagate constraints from anywhere to anywhere, and the devil can exploit this to devise unmanageably intricate instances of the problem. One wonders if there are some reasonable restrictions to prevent this. Are there limitations that can be placed on the SCI graph so that combinatorial constraints generated in one part of the architecture will have to stay somewhat local to the area in which they originate? One candidate device to achieve this is to require the SCI graph to be planar. (Planar graphs are ones that can be drawn on a flat piece of paper without any lines

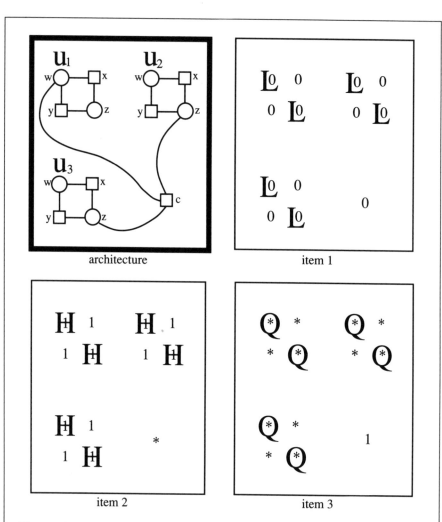

Figure 6.3
Plan view of the composed construction. It uses notation established
in figure 6.2. This example is for the single clause $(u_1, \overline{u_2}, \overline{u_3})$. At top
left is the plan view of the architecture. Node c is a second-layer node
that is used to enforce the disjunctive semantics of the clause. The
three item boxes correspond to items in figure 4.2.

crossing any others.) Unfortunately, the devil that generates loading problems is not sufficiently hampered by this:

THEOREM 16 Loading just those shallow architectures that have planar SCI graphs is *NP*-complete.

Proof[1]: Note one incidental fact about the reduction used in the proof for theorem 15—that the SCI graph for an architecture in that family of constructions is identical to the plan view of the architecture (minus directions on the edges). A similar construction will be used in this theorem; the architecture employed will have a planar plan view and a planar SCI graph simultaneously.

The proof of corollary 15 can be re-employed for the present theorem here so long as it can be arranged for no arcs to cross in the drawing of the SCI graph. The following proof does this in the usual way (see [Lic82]): it shows how to eliminate all crossing arcs without altering how constraints propagate and interact with one another. See the "crossover construct" in figure 6.4.

Let the label in a node in this diagram also denote the value emitted by that node for input 0 1 (input 0 1 is abbreviated as a Q in the item diagram). By comparing item 1 with item 2, deduce that $p \neq 0$ or $p' \neq 0$. By comparing item 4 with item 5, deduce that $p \neq 1$ or $p' \neq 1$. From these it follows that $p \neq p'$. Similarly, by comparing item 2 with item 3, and item 5 with item 6, it follows that $q \neq q'$. Thus p' is a copy (albeit a negative copy) of p, and q' is a (negative) copy of q. The copies can be re-inverted using the construction in figure 6.2b. Thus the information about p and q "pass through each other" in the plane, and the techniques for proving theorem 15 can be used for the present theorem as well.

---

[1]This proof employs a node function set that is not linearly separable and therefore is not directly applicable to the conventional connectionist devices. However, there is a more elaborate construction based on an invention by Lichtenstein [Lic82] that holds for the standard linear threshold functions. See appendix D.

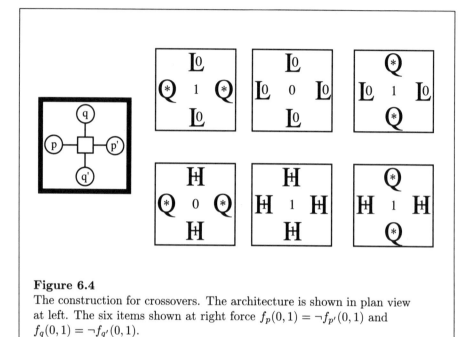

Figure 6.4
The construction for crossovers. The architecture is shown in plan view
at left. The six items shown at right force $f_p(0,1) = \neg f_{p'}(0,1)$ and
$f_q(0,1) = \neg f_{q'}(0,1)$.

Since there are only a polynomial number of crossing points in a
graph, each one can be replaced by the (fixed) amount of extra construction given here, which still yields a polynomial reduction from
3SAT.   □

In spite of this result, intuition is partly right here—it is the interaction of a myriad of constraints that makes things difficult to decide.
Whereas planarity can block the *direct* communication of such constraints, this proof demonstrates that there are *indirect* methods of
propagation that are just as effective. The devil can be just as fiendish
by being a little more devious. So SCI planarity is not a tight enough
constraint to escape *NP*-completeness. In fact, no kind of restriction
on the SCI graph that is vulnerable to 2-dimensional expansion seems
to hold much promise. Define a *grid* as a checkerboard graph on nodes
$x_{i,j}$ where the edges are either $(x_{i,j}, x_{i+1,j})$ or $(x_{i,j}, x_{i,j+1})$.   Figure 6.5

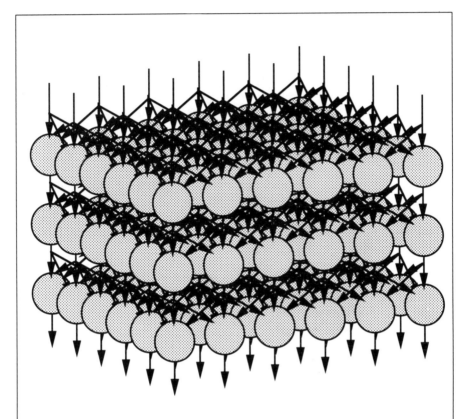

Figure 6.5

A columnar grid architecture. Each node has five inputs from the layer above it—one from the node directly above it and four from the nearest neighbours of that one above. (Nodes around the periphery have fewer inputs.) Each of the three layers shown above is composed of 36 of these units, arranged in a six by six grid.

This structure is an approximate distillation of the structure found in some areas of the brain, although what is shown here would be an extremely small specimen. The complexity questions are concerned with what happens as the specimen gets very much larger.

sketches an architecture that has low and regular depth, low and regular fan-in, and a local and regular connectivity pattern. It is called a
columnar grid because it has a generic column replicated and composed
in such a way that the plan view looks like a 2-dimensional grid. As
usual, the complexity question about these architectures deals with an
infinite family. A family of columnar grids is defined by a depth and a
member of the family is specified by giving the length and width of the
grid. The ability to load regular shallow families like this would pre-
suppose the ability to load that family with the extreme depth of just
2 layers, but for this subcase, and even the following more restrictive
subsubcase, the devil can exact his due. Witness:

THEOREM 17 Loading shallow architectures that have grid SCI graphs
is NP-complete.

Proof: All the individual constructs in figure 6.2b and figure 6.4 can
fit easily into a grid topology. It remains to show how they can all be
connected. For this we need only demonstrate how to transform one
of the arbitrary-shaped and arbitrary-lengthed arcs of figure 6.3 into
an equivalent implication while following grid lines; i.e., how a variable
can be propagated from one point on the grid to most any other point.
Using the construction from figure 6.2b, we can make a negated copy of
a variable in a diagonally adjacent node. Using the construction from
figure 6.4, we can make a negated copy of a variable in a node 2 places
away horizontally or vertically. Using combinations of these, we can
copy a variable either positively or negatively to any other node in the
grid. (See figure 6.6 for examples.) Thus any construction for theorem
16 can be padded with extra nodes until it becomes a grid structure. □

These grid SCI graphs have node degree 4. Loading is also NP-
complete when the SCI graph is a hexagonal array (node degree 3).
Proof omitted. When node degree is limited further to just 2, the SCI
graph becomes a chain and the problem is easy. Proof in the next
section.

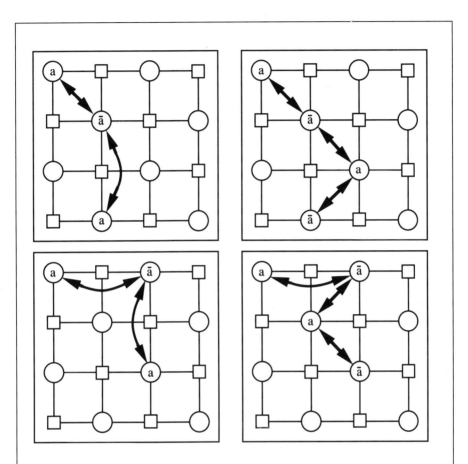

Figure 6.6
Example task designs for propagating variables. Each diagram shows
the plan view of a 2-layer architecture. The dark horizontal and
vertical arrows indicate the effect of the task construct in figure 6.4;
the dark diagonal arrows indicate the effect of the task construct in
figure 6.2b.

These four diagrams illustrate that a variable or its negation can be
propagated throughout a grid architecture from one first-layer node to
any other first-layer node.

6.3   Definitions Again

Definition   Let $\text{DOM}(X)$ denote the domain of the function X. Two configurations F and G are said to be *compatible*, written $F \cong G$, if they have a common extension:

$$F \cong G \Longleftrightarrow \forall v \in \text{DOM}(F) \cap \text{DOM}(G) \quad F(v) = G(v)$$

Note that a partial configuration for node a is trivially compatible with a partial configuration for node b if $sc(a) \cap sc(b) = \emptyset$.

The union of two configurations F and G is defined when $G \cong H$:

$$F = G \cup H \Longleftrightarrow \text{DOM}(F) = \text{DOM}(G) \cup \text{DOM}(H), F \cong G, F \cong H$$

The usual notion of restrictions on functions is also useful:

$$F = G|_A \Longleftrightarrow \text{DOM}(F) = A, \ F \cong G, \ \text{DOM}(G) \supseteq A$$

Definition   A *correct partial configuration*, $\tilde{F}$, for node x is a partial configuration with the property that for any extension of $\tilde{F}$ to a complete configuration F, $\mathcal{M}_F^A$ at node x agrees with the corresponding response bit over all items in the task. A correct partial configuration for a group of nodes contains a correct partial configuration for each node in the group.

Definition   The *bandwidth* of a graph measures the greatest distance that any two adjacent vertices in a graph must be separated when the nodes are strung out in a straight line. Let G be a graph with nodes $V(G)$ and edges $E(G)$. Let a one-to-one function $\ell : V \to \{1, 2, \ldots, |V(G)|\}$ be called a *layout* of G. Then G has bandwidth b if there exists some layout, ℓ, such that for all $(x, y) \in E, |\ell(x) - \ell(y)| \le b$. An example graph and its layout are given in figure 6.7.

Definition   The *armwidth* of a graph is defined by [RS86] in the following way: Let G be a graph. A *tree-decomposition* of G is a family $\mathcal{X} = \{X_i : i \in I\}$ of node-groupings (subsets of $V(G)$), together with a tree D with $V(D) = I$, which have the following properties:

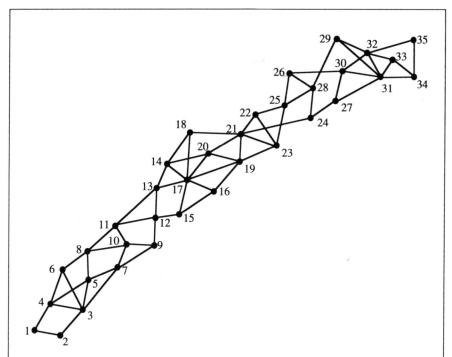

Figure 6.7
An example graph with bandwidth 4. Note that the gross structure is lineal, which could be extended indefinitely without increasing the bandwidth. The layout for the graph is given by the node labels.

- $\bigcup\{X_i : i \in I\} = V(G)$
- Every edge of G has both its ends in X_i for some $i \in I$.
- For $i, j, k \in I$, if j lies on the path in D from i to k then $X_i \cap X_k \subseteq X_j$.

The *width* of a tree-decomposition is $\max\{|X_i| - 1 : i \in I\}$. The *armwidth* of G is the minimum width over all tree-decompositions.[2]

---

[2]The armwidth of a graph is a generalization of bandwidth which I developed (at great effort, alas) and defined in terms of a pebbling game or a vertex-elimination procedure. During preparation of this thesis it was discovered that the notion

As examples of this concept, trees and forests have armwidth ≤ 1, and series-parallel graphs have armwidth ≤ 2. For $n \geq 1$, the complete graph K_n has armwidth $n - 1$, and the $n \times n$ rectangular grid (as in theorem 17) has armwidth n. The bandwidth of a graph is never smaller than its armwidth, but it is known that trees (armwidth 1) have unbounded bandwidth even when their fan-in is limited to 3 [GGJK78]. Figure 6.8 shows an example graph that has armwidth 4. Figure 6.9 shows an example graph that has armwidth 16.

Definition   A *compressed* tree-decomposition is a tree-decomposition where no node-grouping includes any other.

LEMMA 18 In any compressed tree-decomposition $(\mathcal{X}, D)$ for an n-node graph G, the tree D has no more than n nodes.

Proof (by induction on n): It is trivially true for the basis case $n = 1$. Assume it is true for any n, and expand the tree-decomposition by attaching a new node, i, to an existing leaf, j. Since the new X_i is incomparable to X_j, there must be some node, $v_i \in X_i, v_i \notin X_j$. And because all routes out of i go through j, v_i cannot exist in *any* other node-grouping. Hence the number of nodes in G must grow at least as fast as the number of nodes in D.   □

If any good tree-decomposition can be found for a graph, then it is easy to find a compressed one, so it is not an onerous restraint to require that the ones we work with will all be compressed:

LEMMA 19 Given a tree-decomposition $(\mathcal{X}, D)$ for graph G, a compressed tree-decomposition for G can be found in linear time.

---

has been independently developed by others [ACP87, AP88, WHL85, CK87]. The treatment given by Robertson and Seymour [RS86] is more appealing than my definition for the purposes of the proof below, so I use their notation but retain my name for it. In Robertson and Seymour's scheme of things, the name 'tree-width' makes sense. Alas, that word has a different and widely accepted meaning, and it is helpful to give the idea a separate and more immediately intuitive name. My definition can be found in a technical report [Jud88a] proving its equivalence to "embeddings in partial k-trees" and "tree-width."

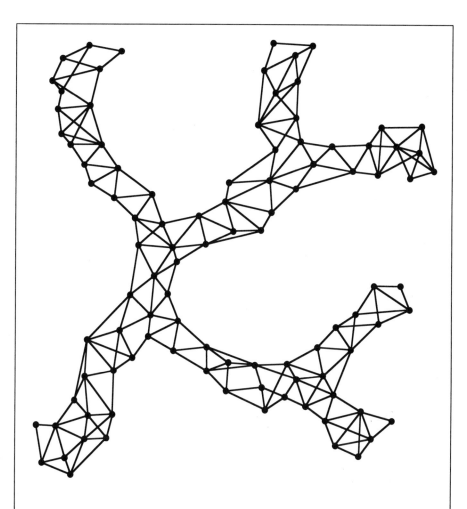

Figure 6.8

An example graph with armwidth 4. Its bandwidth is approximately
16. Note that the gross structure is a tree, but each arm in this tree is
not a simple path graph as a true tree would have, but is a "fatter"
structure. Each of these fat arms, taken independently, is a graph with
bandwidth 4.

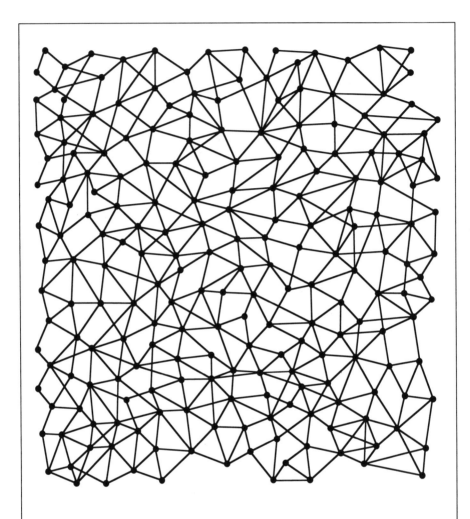

Figure 6.9
An example graph with armwidth 16. Its bandwidth is also 16. It is intended to exemplify graphs that extend more or less uniformly in 2 dimensions.

Proof: Let $\mathcal{X} = \{X_1, X_2, \ldots\}$. If any X_k is contained in some X_i, then it is contained by X_j where j is adjacent to k (in D), and is on the path from k to i. Remove k from D; connect all its other neighbors to j; and discard X_k from $\mathcal{X}$. This does not introduce any new nodes on the path between any two nodes of D, nor does it alter the width of the decomposition. It is sufficient to check and repeat this operation (if necessary) once for every edge in D. In linear time a new tree-decomposition will be found where every pair of node-groupings is incomparable. □

6.4 Armwidth Constraints

The theorems above deal with constrained families of architectures and assert that the loading problem is intractable for those families. This section examines a different type of constraint and reports polynomial-time (viz., tractable) algorithms for them.

We begin with an example family of networks called columnar lines. These architectures are described graphically in figure 6.10a. They are of some fixed depth (4 in the example shown) and of unbounded width, so they qualify as a shallow family. Their fish-net pattern of connectivity gives rise to the family of SCI graphs depicted in figure 6.10b. Regardless of the width of the architecture, its SCI graph has a bandwidth (and armwidth) of 3 (one less than the depth of the net).

Observation: Loading columnar line architectures is polynomial.

Proof sketch: Create a graph with a collection $h_1, h_2, h_3, \ldots$ of sets of nodes, where a node h_k^i stands for the ith correct partial configuration for the support cone of the kth output node. Then add edges (h_k^i, h_{k+1}^j) whenever $h_k^i \cong h_{k+1}^j$. This *compatability graph* represents all the mutually acceptable partial configurations for intersecting support cones. See figure 6.11 for an example. A solution to the loading problem corresponds to a connected path from some member of h_1 to some member of h_2 to some member of h_3 and so on to the end. Finding such a path requires only polynomial time. □

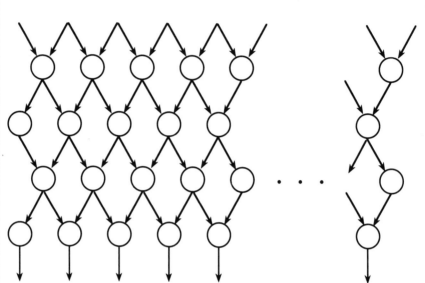

(a) The family of columnar line architectures (of depth 4) shown in classic side view. At right is a single 'column' and on the left is a sample of 5 columns joined together. An architecture in this family is composed of any number of such columns joined in the manner shown.

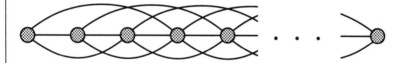

(b) The SCI graph for the columnar line architecture of (a) above. Each node corresponds to an output node of the architecture. Arcs occur wherever their associated support cones overlap. Regardless of the length of this graph, it has bandwidth 3.

Figure 6.10
Columnar line architectures and their SCI graphs

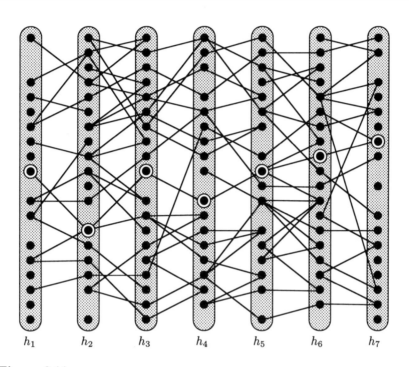

h_1 h_2 h_3 h_4 h_5 h_6 h_7

Figure 6.11

An example compatability graph for a lineal architecture with seven
output nodes. This very simple sort of structure where support cones
intersect only their two adjacent neighbours would arise in a columnar
line of depth two.

Each grey oblong encompasses the set of correct partial configurations
for one of the output nodes. Each black dot represents a correct partial
configuration, and the lines represent compatabilities between them.
The compatability graph is related to the SCI graph but has another
level of detail.

A correct total configuration for the network corresponds to a
continuous line from left to right through this graph, e.g., following the
highlighted dots.

The next theorem generalizes this observation.

THEOREM 20 Loading shallow architectures whose SCI graphs are of limited armwidth can be accomplished in polynomial time, provided that a compressed tree-decomposition is given that exhibits the required width.

Proof: Let D and $\{X_i : i \in V(D)\}$ be the tree-decomposition of the SCI graph. Let $\tau, \tau_1, \tau_2, \dots$ stand for subtrees of D. Let $region(\tau) = \bigcup \{X_i : i \in V(\tau)\}$. Let the set of all correct partial configurations for the group of architectural output nodes corresponding to a group, X, of nodes in the SCI graph be denoted $scpc[X]$. Any member of $scpc[region(D)]$ is a solution configuration. And let the root node of a subtree τ be denoted $root(\tau)$.

The following recursive dynamic programming subroutine has access to an architecture, its SCI graph, and the tree-decomposition for the graph, and it takes some subtree of D as an argument:

```
Solve(τ):
   for every immediate subtree τⱼ of τ
      calculate Sⱼ ← Solve(τⱼ)
   calculate Ŝ ← scpc[X_root(τ)]
   calculate S ← {F̂ : F̂ ∈ Ŝ, ∀j∃Fⱼ ∈ Sⱼ F̂ ≅ Fⱼ}
   return S
```

The claim is that for any given subtree, τ, every member of the returned set $S \leftarrow \text{Solve}(\tau)$ has an extension that is correct for all of τ; and all correct configurations for τ must be extensions of some member of S.

Claim: $\exists \hat{F} \in \text{Solve}(\tau) \iff \exists F \in scpc[region(\tau)] \ \hat{F} = F|_{X_{root(\tau)}}$.

Proof: (by induction on the height of τ) For the basis case where τ is a single leaf node, ℓ, Solve returns $S = \hat{S} = scpc[X_\ell]$ so the claim is true. For the inductive step, assume the claim true for any subtrees $\tau_1, \tau_2, \tau_3, \dots$ and consider a deeper subtree, τ^+, consisting of a root node, h, and subtrees $\tau_1, \tau_2, \tau_3, \dots$ immediately below it. Say $\exists \hat{F} \in \text{Solve}(\tau^+)$. Then $\hat{F} \in scpc[h]$, and for all j there must be an

$H_j \in$ Solve(τ_j) such that $\hat{F} \cong H_j$, because of the way S is calculated. So $\exists F_j \in scpc[region(\tau_j)]$ and $H_j = F_j|_{X_{root(\tau_j)}}$ by the inductive assumption.

Now by definition of the tree-decomposition, DOM$(H_j) \supseteq$ DOM$(F_j) \cap$ DOM$(\hat{F})$. So $\exists F_j^+ = F_j \cup \hat{F} \in scpc[region(\tau_j) \cup X_h]$. It remains to show that all the F_j^+ are mutually compatible; this must be so because a path from one subtree to any other must pass through the root h. Hence DOM$(F_i^+) \cap$ DOM$(F_j^+) \subseteq$ DOM$(\hat{F})$ for any i, j, and $\exists F^+ = \hat{F} \cup \bigcup_j \{F_j\} \in scpc[region(\tau^+)]$. This proves the $\Rightarrow$ direction.

Conversely, if $\exists F^+ \in scpc[region(\tau^+)]$, then the (exhaustive) algorithm must find $\hat{F} = F^+|_{X_h}$. This completes the $\Leftarrow$ direction and proves the claim. □

To determine if a solution configuration exists for the whole network, run this algorithm:

```
Pick any node in D to be the root
Calculate S ← Solve(D)
If S = ∅ then reject else accept
```

Any member of S indicates the presence of a solution configuration so this algorithm accepts if and only if the task is performable.

Finally, it must be shown that the running time, $g(n)$, of this algorithm is polynomial. The overall running time is a simple product

$$g(n) = g_1(n) \times g_2(n),$$

where g_1 is the number of invocations of Solve and g_2 is the running time of the straight-line code in the subroutine. The algorithm invokes Solve once per node in the tree, so lemma 18 shows $g_1(n) \leq n$. The other term is $g_2 = O(|scpc[X]|)$, which is exponential in the size of X, but the assumption about armwidth constrains the maximum size of X, so execution time is limited to $g_2 = O(1)$. Hence the total time is $g(n) = n \times O(1) = O(n)$. This finishes the proof of the theorem. □

The running time constants could be markedly improved in the algorithm given here, but note that the running time is *linear* in the size of the architecture and in task size and only gets explosive when the armwidth (and per force the bandwidth) grows. This problem can therefore be added to the list [MS81, CES81] of *NP*-complete problems that become easier with diminishing bandwidth. (However, the bandwidth characterization may now be irrelevant there, because it seems all of those results can be strengthened by being recast in terms of the weaker notion of armwidth.)

Note that theorem 20 holds even if we loosen the definition of shallow architectures so that the largest *sccs* size is polynomial in n (as opposed to being a constant). In such a case, $g_2(n)$ is polynomial and so is $g(n) = O(n \times g_2(n))$.

Theorem 20 also refers to "limited" armwidth and was worded to imply "limited by a constant", but this is over-strong. Consider a family of architectures characterized only by a growth function $G(n)$ for the armwidth of its SCI graph. The theorem is worded for the case $G(n) = O(1)$, but it would hold true for the case $G(n) = O(\log n)$ because g_2 is only exponential in $G(n)$, which means that it would be polynomial in n. So g would still be polynomial as well.

Now remember that when $G(n) = O(n)$ the loading problem is *NP*-complete (since this is a nonconstraint—the armwidth of *any* graph of n nodes is at most n). These bounds leave a gap between $O(\log n)$ and $O(n)$, which can be narrowed somewhat:

THEOREM 21 For shallow architecture families with a growth function for the armwidth of their SCI graph $G(n) = \Omega(n^\epsilon)$ where ϵ is any positive constant, loading is *NP*-complete.

Proof: Take an arbitrary instance of 3SAT and perform the reduction as in theorem 15. Consider the graph defined on the 3SAT instance, which has a node for every variable, a node for every clause, and edges connecting variable nodes to all the clause nodes they participate in. If this graph is of size n and armwidth w (and $w \leq n$ always), then the constructed instance of loading will have size $O(n)$ and armwidth w.

Now pad the construction with enough isolated nodes to bring it up to size $n' = G^{-1}(n)$. This will not change the armwidth of the loading instance but it will ensure that $w \leq G(n')$, thus satisfying the criterion for membership in the family. Since G is polynomial, G^{-1} is also, so there is only a polynomial amount of padding to do. No matter how small ϵ is, as long as it is greater than 0 there is a polynomial-sized reduction from SAT to loading.   □

This narrowed window of bounds hangs on the armwidth constraint alone and is therefore common to many combinatorial search problems, not just the loading problem.

The following table summarizes our armwidth results and suggests that the complexity of the loading problem is necessarily exponential in the armwidth of the network:

armwidth growth function, $G(n)$	complexity class
constant	linear
logarithmic	polynomial
polynomial, e.g. $n^{0.01}$	NP-complete

Theorem 20 stipulates that the tree-decomposition of the SCI graph must be given as input to the problem because, in general, determining minimum armwidth is an NP-complete problem in itself [ACP87]. This is probably not a problem for connectionists because the network design methodologies we hope to find would presumably be amenable to easy a priori structural analysis. (Assume the network does not change its connectivity during use.) However, if theorem 20 were to be exploited in a direct implementation, it does imply that the nodal learning rules would have to be aware of the structure of the SCI graph, i.e., knowledge of the tree-decomposition would have to be "wired in" to the network somehow.

6.5   Depth and Complexity

By limiting the size of the sccs in all theorems above, we have finessed the whole issue of how the loading problem gets more difficult with depth. This trick has allowed us to focus on the issues arising from expansion of the width of an architecture. But putting individual limits on the *sccs* size and on the armwidth is unnecessarily strong. The real constraint required by the proof of theorem 20 is only that the *scpc* for any node-grouping, X_i, be calculable in a polynomial amount of time.

The possibility of there being an efficient method to search for correct partial configurations has been completely ignored here. One of the quiet payoffs of focusing on shallow architectures is that we could afford to dismiss this particular inquiry as being a "depth issue." The algorithms have been constructed simply to enumerate all possibilities within a support cone, and although this largesse may seem grotesque, it only affects a *linear* constant in the running time.

It is because of this low-complexity interface that the compartmentalization and separation of depth issues from width issues seems to be justified. However it is obvious that someone must get around to examining the depth issues.

6.6   Neural Relevance

It is typically the style of connectionists to adopt a "neural" learning rule and then twist and bend its application until it solves something interesting. This has not been the approach here. The algorithms given above are for the sole purpose of demonstrating that the time complexity of a problem is polynomial. They are not intended to have any neural plausibility; rather I am searching for computational plausibility in the behavioral description of neural machinery. Now it does no good just to describe associative learning at the black box level, nor to describe it at the level of weight-twiddling rules because these things are both easy to come by and neither of these are explicit about the distributed nature of neural computation. The useful description sits at a level intermediate between the outward behavior of the neuron and the outward behavior of the network.

In this chapter I attempted to find a plausible description of that behavior through manipulating aspects of architecture. Fixed-depth architectures were chosen for study partly due to their being easy enough to analyze, but they are of independent interest because of a possible correspondence with cortical structures. Certain parts of the brain (e.g., visual cortex [HW79]) are quite shallow compared to their great width, and the direction of information flow is predominantly unidirectional along the shallow axis. Connections are more or less localized in 3D space surrounding a neuron. Of course real cortical structures are complicated by many connections and other specifics not modeled here, but the process of developing a theory of how such structures work is facilitated by analyzing a few judicious constraints at a time. Most of the constraints chosen here are an approximation to what seem to be the major computational aspects of some cortical structures.

The major exception to this is the armwidth constraint, which does not seem to have any clear reflection in biology at all. It was introduced only because it was the weakest imaginable condition that would force the loading problem in shallow architectures to be polynomial. Logarithmic vs polynomial armwidth feels like it closely characterizes the distinction between polynomial and *NP*-complete problems. But having identified this quantity, we must judge whether it leads to a promising theory of neural computation or whether it is a wrong turn. Two or three biologists have seen neuroanatomical phenomena reflected in the tree structure of figure 6.8 and have wondered whether these were nature's concessions to the loading problem. However, because I am only slightly educated on neuroanatomy, I will trust my own judgment over theirs and reject such a hypothesis as too hopeful. My taste says that the spreading 2-dimensionality of figures 6.5 and 6.9 is a much more characteristic description of how real neural support cones interact, and my hunch is that there are better ways to exorcise *NP*-completeness than to try to fit reality to a theory requiring low armwidth in the SCI graph.

We are still ahead of them, ...
man is still the most extraordinary computer of all.
—*J. F. Kennedy*

Chapter 7

Memorization and Generalization

There are not many joys in human life equal to the joy
of the sudden birth of a generalization.
—*Prince Peter Alekseyvich Kropotkin*

One would hesitate to use neural networks just to memorize and store data because it is probably not economical at all—there are many other engineering techniques that are strong competitors for that honor. But one common motivation for studying neural networks is that they seem to extrapolate their learned knowledge to other parts of their domains that they have not had access to, thereby performing something of great value beyond mere storage. Many people have high hopes for the abilities of neural networks to perform such generalization.

The issue of generalization is not my primary concern here. However, success in generalizing presupposes the ability to memorize simple associative data faithfully and efficiently, and therefore generalization is at least as hard as memorization, which is intractable. Before the issue of generalization can be addressed, the memorization problem must first be solved; hence the results about memorization have a direct bearing on the other issue.

Following are several statements of the same idea; the reader who accepts any one of the arguments might skip the others.

Statement 1   We have found that a network cannot always remember all the items that is has seen. One should therefore not expect it to always be able to extend its knowledge to things it has not seen.

Statement 2   When specifying what is meant by "generalization," one could require that the chosen function agree in all places with the given data, or one might allow some degree of deviation from the given data. In the case where the allowed generalizations must all be consistent with the given task, our results are directly applicable, showing that consistency is, in general, too hard to reliably achieve. The business of finding regularities in data and generalizing from them depends totally on the embedded problem of simply remembering data.

Statement 3   In the case where the application could tolerate 'generalizations' that need not be completely consistent with the given data, our results are sometimes less directly relevant. But corollary 13 is strong enough to apply to some such situations: Even if you allow a loading system to alter the responses on anything less than one third of the items (allowing the system to select which items and what to change them to), it is still *NP*-complete to achieve consistency with the rest.

Statement 4   When one is given a small sampling of items and asked to find a configuration that is consistent with those items, there are typically a vast number of candidate configurations. The notion of "good" generalization corresponds to making an "appropriate" selection from among this field of options. The definition of "appropriate" is of course going begging here. But our *NP*-completeness theorems indicate that it is too difficult to identify even a *single* configuration from this field of candidates. Hence the definition of "appropriate" is of little concern. Regardless of how one might prefer to define generalization, consistency is the nub of the problem.

Statement 5   A system that learns and generalizes from what it learns is often treated in a two-phase experimental paradigm. The first phase is called the training phase, and in it some subset of items is selected (by the experimenter) from a task and presented to the system. The second phase is called the testing phase. In it some subset of items (presumably disjoint from the training set) is selected from the task and the system is asked to induce what the responses should be. Of course the performance of the system will be sensitive to how representative the training set is of the overall task and how complete it is. Also, it will be sensitive to how representative the testing set is of the overall task. Among the community using this paradigm there is a widely held meta-theorem which says that the better a system does on the training set, the better it will do on the test set. And this observation would have us concentrate on solving the memorization problem; poor performance in memorization bodes for poor performance in generalization.

Statement 6 The representativeness of the training set and the representativeness of the testing set are very subjective quantities. Hence the two-phase experimental paradigm can give erratic and nonrigorous results. Valiant's definition of learnability has an ingenious mechanism for handling all of these quantities in a standard mathematical way that utilizes a probabilistic criterion of success in learning and generalization. See figure 3.2, page 29. Rather than arbitrarily choosing a training set in advance (which is open to many vagaries and biases), he selects a training set by randomly choosing items according to some unknown a priori distribution over them. Hence the make-up of the training set is objective, albeit probabilistic, and it is biased only by the distribution. He also selects a testing set in the same way, for the same reason. And since the same distribution is used in both cases, the training set is an unbiased sampling of the testing set (and vice versa). Furthermore, the size of the training set is not determined by the experimenter either—it becomes a decision of the algorithm how many items to sample. The testing set is in effect the whole task, but each item is weighted by its relative probability.

The definition then requires that the system usually be correct for most items in the test set. "Usually" is defined by a confidence probability parameter, δ, and "most" is defined by an accuracy probability parameter, ϵ. This definition is often referred to as "PAC-learning" where the acronym stands for "probably almost correct". The criterion of success requires that the learning algorithm terminate in time that is polynomial in $1/\delta$ and $1/\epsilon$ for any given $\delta, \epsilon > 0$. This affords the algorithm a bigger budget of time (and therefore samples) whenever more confidence or more accuracy is desired.

This definition has been examined by Blumer et al. [BEHW87], and they prove that the probability that all consistent hypotheses have error at most ϵ is larger than $1 - (1 - \epsilon)^m r$, where m is the number of samples and r is the number of hypotheses in the space of all hypotheses. This again is an endorsement of consistency; if you can be true to the training set, you will be true to the testing set.

Statement 7 I have utilized Valiant's ϵ, δ ploy directly in a definition of generalization for networks given in figure 7.1. Using this definition, we might ask if the class, $\mathcal{A}$, of all networks can "generalize":

COROLLARY 22 Networks cannot generalize.

Proof: Use the same construction as in theorem 1. Set $\epsilon < 1/3$, and let D be uniform over the three items. Then with probability $\geq 1-\delta$ the algorithm, B, must find a configuration that is consistent with all three of the items. This implies that B will be a probabilistic polynomial-time algorithm for 3SAT, which implies 3SAT $\in RP$.[1] Assuming $RP \neq NP$,[2] this is impossible.   □

---

[1]The complexity class RP is defined as the set of decision problems that have algorithms that run in time polynomial in n and $1/\delta$ and if the answer is NO will always return 0, and if the answer is YES will return 1 with probability $\geq 1 - \delta$.

[2]It is recommended that you assume $RP \neq NP$. Like the conundrum $P \neq NP$ it has not been proved yet, but it is good for your theorebellum to believe it is true.

$\mathcal{A}$ is a design class of architectures.

A is an architecture.

p is a polynomial.

B is an algorithm.

ϵ, δ are probabilities.

F, G are configurations for A.

$\mathcal{M}_F^A$ is the behavior of A when configured with F.

$T \subseteq \{(\sigma, \rho) | \mathcal{M}_F^A(\sigma) = \rho\}$ is a task.

D is a probability distribution over task items.

"$\mathcal{A}$ can generalize" $\iff$ $\begin{cases} (\exists p, B) \text{ such that } (\forall A \in \mathcal{A})(\forall F \text{ for } A) \\ (\forall T \subseteq \mathcal{M}_F^A)(\forall D \text{ over } T)(\forall \epsilon, \delta > 0) \\ B \text{ halts in time } p(|A|, |T|, 1/\epsilon, 1/\delta) \text{ with} \\ \text{output } G \text{ that with probability } \geq 1 - \delta \\ \text{has property } \sum_{\{(\sigma,\rho) \in T : \mathcal{M}_G^A(\sigma) \neq \rho\}} D(\sigma) < \epsilon \end{cases}$

Figure 7.1

A definition of generalization in networks

Statement 8 I am not claiming that useful generalization can never be performed by connectionist networks. But what I do claim is that the consistency problem is a *prior* consideration. If simple consistency cannot be achieved when required (at least for the target family of tasks), then it is premature to worry about making predictions for unseen stimuli.

Chapter 8

Conclusions

A man is infinitely more complicated than his thoughts.
—*Paul Valéry*

8.1 Lessons Drawn from Current Results

Loading is hard: The job of simply remembering associated pairs of strings requires only linear time in a von Neumann machine, but we have shown that a large-scale version of this trivial problem can become very difficult if it must be achieved in a given nonrecurrent network. Hence there is reason for connectionist research to find out why this phenomenon occurs and how to avoid it. The scale-up problem will not be solved without a deeper understanding of the issues involved in learning, and this entails the development of narrower definitions for the kinds of learning we want to achieve.

Neural networks have been touted as having more natural and more powerful learning abilities than traditional AI learning systems. Certainly, there is some appeal and basis for the argument. It is more comfortable to believe that a small adjustment to a few weights in a net will (a) create a new behavior that is substantially like the old behavior, and (b) quite possibly improve the behavior. In contrast, a small adjustment to a few bits in the program of a Turing Machine will (a) usually produce radically different behavior, and (b) often produce a totally useless behavior. Whether this argument is fair or not fair, this book has demonstrated that before we can harness this quality of gentle adaptations, we still need to know a lot more about the network model, how to design it, how to program it, and what applications to put it to.

Issues of Node Function Sets: A significant set of side questions arose during my research regarding the justification and appropriateness of the type of node functions typically used in the connectionist literature:

- Is there any support for the choice of node function sets that use linear summing techniques? Why use LSFns? or LLFns? Why not?
- Can learning theory speak to the issue?
- Are some node function sets easier to learn with than others?

We have good evidence that the difficulty of the loading problem is independent of the choice of type of functions that each node can perform. For all reasonable sets, our results are completely independent of the choice of node function set; hence nothing in this work either supports or detracts from the use of the currently popular node functions LSFns and LLFns.

As mentioned near the end of chapter 4, Blum and Rivest [BR88] have found a different proof of the NP-completeness of $Perf_{LSFns}$ and their argument depends directly on having to linearly separate many points in s-space. If the three nodes in their construction were using AOFns, LUFns, or some other functions instead of LSFns, the proof would not hold. Hence the only evidence from learning complexity uncovered so far speaks somewhat *against* linear summing! However this is a quite weak argument as it stands—there is no need to abandon linear sums yet.

That our results are independent of the node function set means that the complexity of loading does not derive from the node function set. What it does derive from is the connectivity patterns of the network. This much is clear. Notwithstanding, there is a great deal of research effort being put into understanding linear threshold functions and also into studies of linear threshold networks. For instance Minsky and Papert [MP72] treat linear threshold devices as a primary issue. This is reasonable strategy for investigating the power of small networks; indeed in the case of tiny networks (i.e., one node or one layer), the role of the node function set is ascendant because it has an overwhelming effect on what can be performed by the net. In large or deep networks, the role of the node function set in determining computational power fades quickly and is replaced by issues like the size, depth, and connectivity of the net. This suggests, therefore, that studies of linear threshold devices, if not totally irrelevant to learnability, are at least guilty of placing undue importance on an issue that will only help settle minor issues. See also [MP72, footnote, page 165].

Generalization: Although generalization properties are exciting possibilities for neural networks, several arguments have been made that the simple issue of consistency is a central and prior consideration. Good generalization requires good memorization.

Design Constraints: It has been shown that loading can be hard, that it can be easy, and that one of the things this depends on is the family of architectures being loaded. The theorems serve as warnings and as guideposts to better designs. When the SCI of a shallow architecture has limited armwidth, loading is tractable, but this constraint may not yield useful families of networks. Less constrained families that we looked at (e.g. grid SCI graphs) have *NP*-complete loading problems. These results are some evidence that architectural constraints alone will not serve as a useful exit from *NP*-completeness. Other aspects of the problem will need to be changed, possibly in conjunction with architectural constraints.

Methodology: A wide range of questions have been outlined regarding narrowed or altered models of the connectionist learning goal. The particular subcases considered here are merely a few of the myriad avenues open for research. The tool of *NP*-completeness can direct the search for good learning rules and/or easily loaded architectures and/or easily loaded tasks without requiring extensive simulations. By carefully refining definitions and searching for a more complete description of the boundary between solvable and infeasible problems, a more useful theory will develop that will have applications to the design of many kinds of network machines.

8.2   Contributions of this Book

We have focused on the scale-up problem in supervised learning as an area requiring major effort and applied standard tools of complexity theory to try to understand it.

The first major contribution made in this research program is to have identified and formalized the basic computational problem underlying the connectionist learning problem. There are four little parts that went into its construction.

1. The five-step cycle of classical connectionist learning (which took a stimulus and response and produced a weight change—see section 2.5) was condensed into taking a task into a configuration of weights.

2. The notion of a node function set was generalized so that we stopped referring to a configuration *of weights* and simply referred to a configuration.

3. The distributed nature of the classical algorithms was removed and supplanted by serial computation.

4. The architecture was made into an explicit input.

Altogether, this gave us the form of the loading problem as a function from (architecture, task) pairs to configurations. This computational question has been demonstrated here to be of broad general value in finding design constraints for neural networks. There is a very large class of related questions that follow the basic formulation but particularize it by stating restrictive definitions on the various aspects of the problem. Although formalizations of problems often look straightforward and easy in hindsight, the development of the formulation itself represents a considerable component of this thesis.

Complementing this formulation is the recognition of its relationship to other models of learning given by Valiant and Gold.

In their book *Perceptrons* [MP72], Minsky and Papert lament the lack of an effective procedure for loading networks and express a hope that "some profound reason for the failure to produce an interesting learning theorem for the multilayered machine will be found." This thesis supplies such a reason, and the proofs of its theorems stand as opening insights into the reasons why the loading problem is so difficult. The fact that network learning is *NP*-complete may not be surprising in itself, but its proof is still a valuable contribution on its own.

In penetrating the issues surrounding expansion of network width, the notions of shallowness and SCI graphs have been developed and their usefulness has been demonstrated while pursuing the distinction between polynomial and *NP*-complete problems.

This work also raised the question of how we might justify linear sum functions in networks or find another node function set that might be more appropriate for learning.

Prompted by that question, good evidence appeared that the difficulty of the loading problem does not derive from features of the node function set. In fact the theorems find no evidence in support of any node function set over any other. Perhaps this is a nonresult; or perhaps it argues that good research strategy should ignore the particularities of any one node function set and concentrate instead on higher-level issues.

It has been shown why the development of a theory of learning in networks would directly contribute to the otherwise black art of network design. Numerous further avenues have been identified that would study the effect of scale-up on the learning issue and thereby derive principles that contribute to a methodology of network design.

Last, the notion of armwidth (aka tree-width and partial k-trees) has been developed. This idea is useful well beyond the borders of this study and deserves wide exposure to graph theorists and algorithm designers. It characterizes an important metric on graphs and leads to polynomial subcases for otherwise *NP*-complete problems. Indeed, other researchers have independently discovered the same notion, and papers on the topic have now appeared in the literature.

8.3   Future Work

The obvious extensions to this work include refining the classes of architectures considered and the classes of tasks considered, so as to more closely understand the relationship between networks and what they can learn. Some specific directions are outlined in the following.

Task Constraints

Although this study has focused on what it expressed as *architectural* design issues, these results could just as easily have been expressed as *task* design issues; in fact they are both. Whenever we found poly-time loadable architectures, we were also implicitly identifying poly-time loadable tasks, since the class of tasks that such architectures were capable of loading was given as the set of all tasks performable by that architecture. Hence the investigation has had dual purpose throughout. However, it is a limitation of this work that we have generally inquired only about the ability of a network to load *all* of its performable tasks instead of asking about its ability to load some useful subset of its performable tasks. This should be explored further.

To pursue such questions, one needs to identify interesting classes of tasks and find useful formal definitions for them. In section 5.2 we used a target-net/learner formalism to constrain the class of tasks a network might be asked to load. This technique was used only in conjunction with differing node function sets, but it is also useful in other contexts. For example, it might be useful to be able to describe exactly what tasks an architecture is capable of learning by referring to a target-net network whose tasks it can easily load. As before, denote this by writing the parameters for describing the target-net to the left of *Perf* and those for the learner to the right. For example the question as to whether network A' could learn all of what network A could perform would be $^A Perf^{A'}$. Is there a reasonable ϕ function from architectures to architectures such that for all A, $^A Perf^{\phi(A)}$ is tractable?

This question can be answered positively. When given a network, A, and any task of t items, one can construct a network approximately t times as big as A that can easily load that task. This is a crude upper bound on the size of learner network required; and because the factor is t rather that some power of t or some exponential in t, it seems that tighter answers to the ϕ question might indeed be interesting.

The purpose of the target-net/learner formalism is to unbundle the architecture class from the task class and to deal with them explicitly and independently.

Relaxed Criteria

The basic loading problem asked for a *guarantee* that the algorithm would complete its job of finding a configuration. It might be that some probabilistic criterion of success would be easier to comply with. Perhaps for some class of architectures we will be able to find a randomized procedure that will run in polynomial time and report a solution configuration with a certain minimum probability. Repeated invocations of the procedure would give asymptotic certainty regarding performability. Such an algorithm could be used in applications where it was possible to judge how much loading time each situation warranted.

Mutating the Network

Another avenue of freedom usually not exploited by connectionist learning schemes is to alter the architecture as learning proceeds. When carried to extremes, this would amount to an exercise in circuit design, for which Valiant's formulation of the learning problem is the most relevant. This is a far cry from current approaches to connectionist learning, but adhering rigidly to the starting architecture may be too constrictive; somewhere between these two extremes may be a scheme that combines the best of both approaches.

Modularization

The difficulties inherent in connectionist learning may be manageable through some notion of network modularization. The general idea is to bring circuit-design principles into the connectionist arena at a very high level (i.e. by specifying gross structure of the network to match something about the underlying problem), and leave lower details (i.e. about contributions of individual nodes) to the learning rules. Many researchers have experimented with such an approach, although it is still quite unclear how to harness it.

Returning to Classical Form

As discussed in section 2.6, the loading problem is on the easy side of three issues, and therefore whenever a tractable loading problem is identified, we do not have complete evidence that the problem will be easy in the classical connectionist setting. For such a case we would still have three aspects to adapt, all of which would require a special research effort since none of them are well understood:

- The type of machine used: The serial algorithm would have to be broken up and distributed throughout the network.
- The style of processing required: The process would have to be re-implemented in a 'neural' style.
- The type of information available: The system would have to be altered to accept information in an on-line fashion.

Recurrent Networks

This book has specifically focused on feed-forward networks. Recurrent networks have a fundamentally different retrieval process in that they start at some point in state space and under the influence of the input they travel through state space, possibly reaching a stable point or a limit cycle. The definition of what constitutes its "output" may therefore be problematical, but this sort of machine is very interesting and the problem of loading them should be studied. Shallow feed-forward models might be relevant to (long-term) storage of information in the brain, but hypotheses about short-term memory in the brain are often based on cyclic electrical mechanisms that require recurrent networks.

Other Learning Paradigms

This work has been limited to the supervised learning paradigm. Many other types of protocols (e.g., unsupervised learning, helpful teachers, or the use of queries) are useful models of learning environments but have not been formally explored in the context of learning in networks.

Deep Networks

The effect of depth on loading complexity is one issue that has been consistently suppressed in this work. Protected by asymptotic arguments, our theorems have brazenly thumbed their noses at the problems inherent in very deep networks. But this is thin protection—no realistic implementation could afford to run exhaustive searches of all configurations for any useful-sized support cone. Any useful theory of loadability will have to understand this issue.

The following computational problem is offered as a loading problem that might capture the crux of depth difficulties. Readers are invited to determine whether or not it is *NP*-complete.

Instance: An integer and a task.

Question: The integer gives the depth (and width) of an architecture depicted in figure 8.1. The nodes are arranged in a triangle with each layer having one fewer nodes than the previous layer until the last layer has one node in it. Each node receives an input from both of the two above it. The task is a collection of items, each with $d+1$ stimulus bits and 1 response bit. Is there a configuration for this architecture that performs the given task?

Use whatever node function set you happen to fancy. (For two-input gates it hardly matters.)

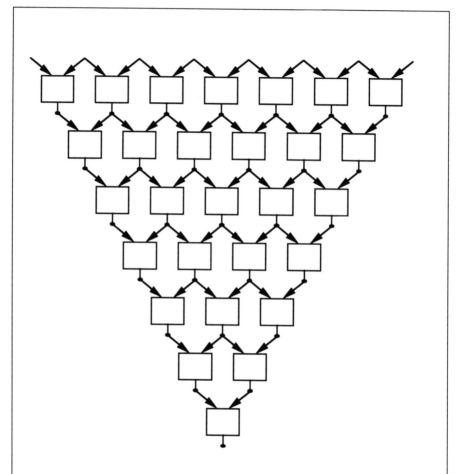

Figure 8.1
A triangular architecture for a depth problem. This is the prototypical
shape of members of an infinite family of architectures. The family is
meant to capture one systematic way of expanding the size of a support
cone and thus set up a formal question about loading deep networks.

8.4 Philosophical Summary

A theory is developed by progressing from one hard, clear definition of a problem to another. Clearly, what connectionists require of a learning system is still ill defined. There are many formulations of it other than the one used here that might be appropriate for different situations. It may be reasonable just to ask for the "best" configuration for a network, rather than the "correct" configuration. It may be reasonable just to ask for the configuration that yields performance better than a simple regression procedure would. It may be reasonable just to ask for a configuration that makes maximal use of the hardware (i.e., supports the greatest number of items in the given network). The contribution of such research may be to help define connectionist learning by showing which formulations are achievable. The loading problem is a basic model; other formulations based on more refined definitions could lead to successively more useful models of practical connectionist concerns. Because no exact definitions of connectionist learning are yet widely accepted, it may be that an analysis of various definitions leading to tractable loading problems would help establish and focus the research in this area.

The successful development of a theory of an intensely complicated system like the brain depends on a judicious sequence of selections of constraints. To begin, one must select one or two appropriate constraints, then study them to understand how they interact, choose another constraint, then add it to the others and elaborate further. At each choice point, one must be carefully conscious of what level of detail the system is being modeled at and choose constraints that act at that same level. It is arguable that there has been too much emphasis placed on modeling brains at the level of neurons using constraints like spike train frequencies, linear threshold functions, or the sodium pump. Such research might turn out to be as inefficient as trying to discover the principles of flight by studying the microbiology of birds. The useful study occurs at a level much coarser than microbiology. Similarly here, just by taking a view from the next larger scale of detail, our investigations have discovered a universe of issues that are almost oblivious to the functionality of individual nodes. This suggests that these coarser levels of detail will be more productive levels of modeling for computer scientists to pursue. It could well be that after a theory of learnability is fleshed out, tuning it for a specific node function set will change things only slightly. In general the coarser levels of description are the more important levels.

What was attempted herein was to look at the level of mid-size neuroanatomical structures (e.g., cortical slabs), and it is hoped that our choice of simple constraints will prove propitious. We have explored feed-forward networks and especially the architectural family of shallow networks because of their potential for modeling structures in natural brain cortex. The model will be relevant if we have been lucky in choosing constraints and if the neural structures they model also happen to be engaged in the kind of information loading and retrieval that we are studying. We might have the wrong model of the salient aspects of these slabs of cortical columns; we might have the wrong model of how these slabs actually retrieve their stored information; or we might just be asking the wrong analytical question. (The performability problem requires total, exact, dependable recognition of the set of performable tasks. This seems unduly demanding, and of the three suspicions listed here, this last one seems to deserve the first examination.)

Whatever the case, the underlying assumption is that complexity analysis (and specifically the P vs NP distinction) provides a means to narrow down the things that biological machines do and how they do it. Our strategy has been to take the general NP-complete problem and add architectural constraints, task constraints, or other types of constraints, and search for polynomial-time loading problems. Most people feel very safe in claiming that the brain cannot be fully solving any NP-hard problem, and it is also a good bet that evolution would have found efficient ways to utilize the available hardware. Ergo brain mechanisms are likely to be described by decision problems found "just below" the level of NP-completeness. Hence the general outline and thrust of this research program.

By providing guidelines for ensuring that a network can learn efficiently, we will contribute to a sorely needed general methodology of how connectionist networks should be constructed. And by distinguishing between those forms of learning that are achievable and those forms that are not, we will be helping to identify the applications to which neural networks can be profitably applied. This research has provided another few steps toward such a theory.

Informed by neuroscience and computer science,
we can ... begin to discern the shape of a new theory
about the nature of the mind—of what it is for
the physical brain to see, learn, and understand itself;
of what it is to be a human being.
—*Patricia Smith Churchland*

Appendix A

Alternate Proof
of General Theorem

To make a name for learning
When other means are barred,
Take something very easy
And make it very hard.

—Piet Hein

This appendix presents a different proof of the main result. In fact it proves a slightly weaker version of theorem 1 in that it uses a node function set called SAFns, which is larger than AOFns. The next appendix extends this theorem to real-valued node function sets using the same construction used here. SAFns is the set of node functions that can be constructed with a single AND gate augmented with optional inverters at the inputs and output.

First, some general purpose notation for manipulating strings is introduced. If α and β are strings, then $\alpha \cdot \beta$ is the concatenation of α and β, α^n is the concatenation of n copies of α, and $\bigodot_{i=1}^{n} \alpha_i$ denotes $\alpha_1 \cdot \alpha_2 \cdot \alpha_3 \cdot \ldots \cdot \alpha_n$.

If α is a string, A and B are sets (with distinct elements), $B \subseteq A$, and the length of α is $|A|$, then the notation $\alpha[^A_B]$ denotes the string of length $|B|$ that is formed by associating successive elements of α with successive members of A (which has an implicit ordering), and then selecting from α only those elements that are associated with members of B. For example,

$$
\begin{array}{ll}
\text{if} & \alpha = \ 2 \ \cdot 7 \ \cdot 4 \ \cdot 1 \ \cdot 9 \ \cdot \ 8 \\
\text{and} & A = \{d_{10}, d_{14}, d_{15}, d_{16}, d_{17}, d_{19}\} \\
\text{and} & B = \{d_{10}, d_{17}, \ d_{19}\} \\
\hline
\text{then} & \alpha[^A_B] = \ 2 \ \cdot 9 \ \cdot \ 8
\end{array}
$$

Another notational device is used to select single elements from a string; $\alpha\langle k \rangle$ represents the kth element of α. Formally, $\alpha\langle k \rangle = \alpha[^{\{1,2,3,\ldots,a\}}_{\{k\}}]$ where a is the length of α.

For precision, define the semantics of computation in a network as the unique string that satisfies the inductive expression

$$
Comp^A_F(\sigma) = \sigma \cdot \bigodot_{i=1}^{n} f_i(Comp^A_F(\sigma)[^P_{p(v_i)}])
$$

Such a string is unique because A is acyclic and the output of each node is dependent only on the output of previous nodes. The network mapping can now be stated as

$$
\mathcal{M}^A_F(\sigma) = Comp^A_F(\sigma)[^P_R]
$$

THEOREM 23 $Perf_{SAFns}$ is NP-complete.

Proof: We reduce the classic satisfiability problem (SAT) to $Perf_{SAFns}$. (See [GJ79] for an explanation of this process.) Let (U, Γ) be an arbitrary instance of SAT, where U is a set of variables and Γ is a set of clauses; $U = \{u_1, u_2, \ldots u_w\}$, $\Gamma = \{(\gamma_i, G_i) : 1 \leq i \leq m\}$. We use a novel representation of Γ, the set of clauses: for each $i \leq m$, $\gamma_i \in \{0,1\}^w$, and $G_i \subseteq U$. A string Π is said to satisfy the instance (U, Γ) iff $\Pi[^U_{G_i}] \neq \gamma_i[^U_{G_i}]$ for all $i \leq m$. (This representation of a clause can be obtained from the traditional disjunctive form by applying de Morgan's Law once and padding for variables that are not in the clause.)

We must construct an architecture A and a task T such that T is performable by A iff (U, Γ) is satisfiable. The set of nodes V will be composed of a set V_1 of "first-layer nodes" and a set V_2 of "second-layer nodes."

$$S = \{v_{0,i} : 0 \leq i \leq w\}$$

$$V_1 = \{v_{1,j} : 1 \leq j \leq w\}$$

$$V_2 = \{v_{2,i} : 1 \leq i \leq m\}$$

$$P = S \cup V_1 \cup V_2$$

$$R = V = V_1 \cup V_2$$

$$E = \{(v_{0,0}, v_{1,j}), (v_{0,j}, v_{1,j}) : 1 \leq j \leq w\} \cup \{(v_{1,j}, v_{2,i}) : u_j \in G_i\}$$

$$A = (P, V, S, R, E)$$

The task is composed of three kinds of items. The first kind is called the "truth-value items" and associates a binary value with "true" and "false":

$$T_1 = \{(0 \cdot 0^w, 0^w \cdot *^m), (0 \cdot 1^w, 1^w \cdot *^m)\}$$

The second kind of item is called the "disjunct semantics items":

$$T_2 = \{(0 \cdot \gamma_i, *^w \cdot *^{i-1} \cdot 0 \cdot *^{m-i}) : (\gamma_i, G_i) \in \Gamma\}$$

The third kind of item is called the "conjunct semantics item":

$$T_3 = \{(1 \cdot 0^w, *^w \cdot 1^m)\}$$

$$T = T_1 \cup T_2 \cup T_3$$

Figure A.1 gives a construction for an example instance of SAT.

Claim: A solution configuration, F, for (A, T) exists iff a satisfying assignment Π, exists for (U, Γ).

proof ($\exists F \Leftarrow \exists \Pi$): Assume $(U, \Gamma) \in$ SAT by virtue of the satisfying assignment string Π. Associate the node function $f_{k,i}$ with each node $v_{k,i} \in V$, and then let $F = \{f_{1,1}, f_{1,2}, \ldots, f_{1,w}, f_{2,1}, f_{2,2}, \ldots, f_{2,m}\}$ where

Take as an example the following SAT problem expressed in traditional CNF form: $(\overline{u_1} \vee u_2 \vee u_3)(u_2 \vee \overline{u_3} \vee \overline{u_4})$. In the required form, this is equivalent to

$$\gamma_1 = 1 \cdot 0 \cdot 0 \cdot 0 \qquad G_1 = \{u_1, u_2, u_3\}$$
$$\gamma_2 = 0 \cdot 0 \cdot 1 \cdot 1 \qquad G_2 = \{u_2, u_3, u_4\}$$

The task for this problem is

$$\begin{aligned}
T_1 = \quad & (0 \cdot 0 \cdot 0 \cdot 0 \cdot 0, \quad 0 \cdot 0 \cdot 0 \cdot 0 \cdot * \cdot *) \\
& (0 \cdot 1 \cdot 1 \cdot 1 \cdot 1, \quad 1 \cdot 1 \cdot 1 \cdot 1 \cdot * \cdot *) \\
T_2 = \quad & (0 \cdot 1 \cdot 0 \cdot 0 \cdot 0, \quad * \cdot * \cdot * \cdot * \cdot 0 \cdot *) \\
& (0 \cdot 0 \cdot 0 \cdot 1 \cdot 1, \quad * \cdot * \cdot * \cdot * \cdot * \cdot 0) \\
T_3 = \quad & (1 \cdot 0 \cdot 0 \cdot 0 \cdot 0, \quad * \cdot * \cdot * \cdot * \cdot 1 \cdot 1)
\end{aligned}$$

The architecture is as follows:

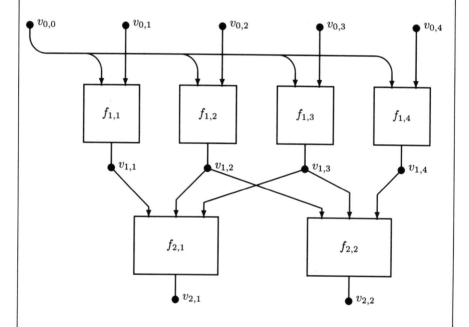

Figure A.1
Example construction for proof using SAFns.

$$f_{1,j}(a \cdot b) = \begin{cases} b & \text{if } a = 0 \\ \Pi\langle j \rangle & \text{if } a = 1 \end{cases}$$

$$f_{2,i}(\alpha) = \begin{cases} 0 & \text{if } \alpha = \gamma_i[^U_{G_i}] \\ 1 & \text{otherwise} \end{cases}$$

We must show that $\mathcal{M}^A_F \supseteq T$, which we do by showing $\mathcal{M}^A_F \supseteq T_1$, $\mathcal{M}^A_F \supseteq T_2$, and $\mathcal{M}^A_F \supseteq T_3$ individually. First, note that since $f_{1,j}(0 \cdot b) = b$ for all $j \leq w$, we have for any α,

$$\begin{aligned}
Comp^A_F(0 \cdot \alpha)[^P_{V_1}] &= \bigodot_{j=1}^{w} f_{1,j}((0 \cdot \alpha)[^S_{p(v_{1,j})}]) \\
&= \bigodot_{j=1}^{w} f_{1,j}(0 \cdot \alpha\langle j \rangle) = \bigodot_{j=1}^{w} \alpha\langle j \rangle = \alpha \qquad \text{(A.1)}
\end{aligned}$$

Equation A.1 proves $Comp^A_F(\sigma)[^P_{V_1}] = \rho[^R_{V_1}]$ for both items $(\sigma, \rho) \in T_1$. Since responses for V_2 are undefined, $\mathcal{M}^A_F \supseteq T_1$.

For each $v_{2,i} \in V_2$ there is only one item in T_2 which is defined, and to agree with that response, we must show that $\mathcal{M}^A_F(0 \cdot \gamma_i)[^R_{V_2}]\langle i \rangle = 0$.

$$\begin{aligned}
\mathcal{M}^A_F(0 \cdot \gamma_i)[^R_{V_2}]\langle i \rangle &= f_{2,i}(Comp^A_F(0 \cdot \gamma_i)[^P_{p(v_{2,i})}]) \\
&= f_{2,i}(Comp^A_F(0 \cdot \gamma_i)[^P_{V_1}][^{V_1}_{p(v_{2,i})}]) \quad \text{since } p(v_{2,i}) \subseteq V_1 \\
&= f_{2,i}(\gamma_i[^{V_1}_{p(v_{2,i})}]) \qquad \text{by (A.1) above} \\
&= f_{2,i}(\gamma_i[^U_{G_i}]) \qquad \text{by definition of } E \\
&= 0 \qquad \text{by definition of } f_{2,i}, \text{ as required.}
\end{aligned}$$

Since this argument holds for every node in V_2, and responses for V_1 are not defined, $\mathcal{M}^A_F \supseteq T_2$.

The only stimulus in T_3 is $1 \cdot 0^w$.

$$\begin{aligned}
Comp^A_F(1 \cdot 0^w)[^P_{V_1}] &= \bigodot_{j=1}^{w} f_{1,j}((1 \cdot 0^w)[^S_{p(v_{1,j})}]) \\
&= \bigodot_{j=1}^{w} f_{1,j}(1 \cdot 0) = \bigodot_{j=1}^{w} \Pi\langle j \rangle = \Pi
\end{aligned}$$

$$Comp^A_F(1 \cdot 0^w)[^P_{V_2}] = \bigodot_{i=1}^{m} f_{2,i}((Comp^A_F(1 \cdot 0^w))[^P_{V_1}][^{V_1}_{p(v_{2,i})}])$$

$$\text{since } \bigcup_{v \in V_2} p(v) \subseteq V_1$$

$$= \bigodot_{i=1}^{m} f_{2,i}(\Pi[^{V_1}_{p(v_{2,i})}]) \qquad \text{by the previous equation}$$

$$= \bigodot_{i=1}^{m} f_{2,i}(\Pi[^U_{G_i}]) \qquad \text{by definition of } E$$

$$= 1^m \qquad \text{by definition of } f_{2,i} \text{ and } \Pi[^U_{G_i}] \neq \gamma_i[^U_{G_i}]$$

So $\mathcal{M}^A_F(1 \cdot 0^w) = \Pi \cdot 1^m \models *^w \cdot 1^m$ which is to say $\mathcal{M}^A_F \supseteq T_3$. This completes the first half of the claim.

proof ($\exists F \Rightarrow \exists \Pi$): Assume $F = \{f_{1,1}, f_{1,2}, \ldots, f_{1,w}, f_{2,1}, f_{2,2}, \ldots, f_{2,m}\}$ is a configuration such that $\mathcal{M}^A_F \supseteq T$. What do we know about F? By inspecting T_1, we know

$$Comp^A_F(0 \cdot 0^w)[^P_{V_1}] = \bigodot_{j=1}^{w} f_{1,j}((0 \cdot 0^w)[^S_{p(v_{1,j})}]) = \bigodot_{j=1}^{w} f_{1,j}(0 \cdot 0) = 0^w$$

by the first item. Hence $f_{1,j}(0 \cdot 0) = 0$. By the second item, we can similarly show $f_{1,j}(0 \cdot 1) = 1$, which leads us to conclude what was shown in equation (A.1).

By inspecting T_2 and T_3, we have for every i, $1 \leq i \leq m$

$$f_{2,i}(Comp^A_F(0 \cdot \gamma_i)[^P_{p(v_{2,i})}]) = 0 \neq 1 = f_{2,i}(Comp^A_F(1 \cdot 0^w)[^P_{p(v_{2,i})}])$$

$$Comp^A_F(0 \cdot \gamma_i)[^P_{p(v_{2,i})}] \neq Comp^A_F(1 \cdot 0^w)[^P_{p(v_{2,i})}]$$

Applying equation (A.1) and the definition of E on the l.h.s.,

$$\text{l.h.s.} = Comp^A_F(0 \cdot \gamma_i)[^P_{V_1}][^{V_1}_{p(v_{2,i})}] = \gamma_i[^{V_1}_{p(v_{2,i})}] = \gamma_i[^U_{G_i}]$$

Simplifying the r.h.s. by letting $\Pi = Comp^A_F(1 \cdot 0^w)[^P_{V_1}]$,

$$\text{r.h.s.} = Comp^A_F(1 \cdot 0^w)[^P_{V_1}][^{V_1}_{p(v_{2,i})}] = \Pi[^{V_1}_{p(v_{2,i})}] = \Pi[^U_{G_i}]$$

Reassembling, we have $\gamma_i[_{G_i}^U] \neq \Pi[_{G_i}^U]$ for all $i, 1 \leq i \leq m$ which is to say that Π satisfies (U, Γ) and the claim is proved.   □

Thus we have SAT $\propto$ $Perf_{SAFns}$, and it is easy to see that the algorithm for the transformation runs in polynomial time (in fact linear time and log space).

Finally, it must be demonstrated that there is a nondeterministic machine that can decide $Perf_{SAFns}$ in time polynomial in the length of (A, T). That is, there must be a polytime method of writing down a valid SAFns configuration and checking that it is correct. Writing down a function from SAFns requires one bit for every nodal input (to specify whether it should be inverted before entering the AND gate) and one bit for the output (to specify whether the whole function should be inverted). For the complete configuration, this takes one bit for each edge in A and one bit for each node in A. That the configuration is correct can be checked by evaluating each node function once for each item in T. This takes time $O(|V| \times |T|)$ under the assumption that it takes constant time to evaluate any single f_i.

This, and SAT $\propto$ $Perf_{SAFns}$ implies $Perf_{SAFns}$ is NP-complete.   □

Appendix B

Proof for Logistic Linear Node Functions

I have yet to see any problem, however complicated,
which, when you looked at it in the right way,
did not become more complicated.
—*Paul Anderson*

The next theorem extends the previous one to the case of certain real-valued node functions. We consider a function set used in [RHW86] wherein every member of the set is a function composed of two parts. The first part is the logistic function and the second is a linear weighted sum of its inputs.

$$f(\alpha) = E(e(\alpha))$$

where $e(\alpha) = w_0 + \sum w_i \times \alpha\langle i \rangle,$

and $E(x) = \dfrac{1}{1 + e^{-x}}.$

We call these functions LLFns (for Logistic Linear Functions). The E function is fixed for all nodes, so to specify a member of LLFns it is enough to specify the weights $w_0, w_1, \ldots$ used in e.

Following [RHW86] again, we say that a value agrees with 1 if it is no smaller than 0.9, and it agrees with 0 if it is no larger than 0.1. Note that $E(x)$ asymptotically approaches 1 as x approaches $+\infty$ and that $E(x)$ asymptotically approaches 0 as x approaches $-\infty$. Let d be some scalar value. We say that α *agrees for high d with* β (written $\alpha \overset{d}{\models} \beta$) if there is some value for d beyond which α always agrees with β. This implies that the value of α or β is a function of d.

$$\alpha(d) \overset{d}{\models} \beta(d) \iff \exists d_0 \text{ such that } \alpha(d) \models \beta(d) \text{ for all } d \geq d_0$$

Such agreement is easy to prove if α is monotonic in d and β is constant.

Note that if two such agreement statements hold for the same high parameter, then they hold simultaneously for that parameter.

$$(\alpha \overset{d}{\models} \beta \text{ and } \delta \overset{d}{\models} \xi) \iff \alpha \cdot \delta \overset{d}{\models} \beta \cdot \xi$$

A new notational device is used to select single elements from a string in the case where the element's position in a string is not known except through its relative position in one of the clause sets, G_i, in Γ.   For that situation, we use $\frac{i}{k}$ to mean the index in U of the kth element of clause i. Formally, $\frac{i}{k} = (\bigodot_{j=1}^{w} j)[_{G_i}^{U}]\langle k \rangle$. Consequently, this identity holds: $\alpha\langle \frac{i}{k} \rangle = \alpha[_{G_i}^{U}]\langle k \rangle$.

THEOREM 24 *Perf*$_{\text{LLFns}}$ is NP-complete.

Proof: We construct a performability problem (A, T) where the architecture, A, is the same as it was in the proof of Theorem 23 except that $R = V_2$ instead of $R = V$, and the task, T, is as follows:

$$T = T_1 \cup T_2 \cup T_3$$

$$T_1 = \{(0 \cdot \gamma_i, \quad *^{i-1} \cdot 0 \cdot *^{m-i}) : 1 \leq i \leq m\}$$

$$T_2 = \{\{(0 \cdot \gamma_i^{(k)}, \quad *^{i-1} \cdot 1 \cdot *^{m-i}) : 1 \leq k \leq |G_i|\} : 1 \leq i \leq m\}$$

$$T_3 = \{(1 \cdot \gamma_i, \quad *^{i-1} \cdot 1 \cdot *^{m-i}) : 1 \leq i \leq m\}$$

where $\gamma_i^{(k)}$ is γ_i with the kth relevant bit inverted:

$$\gamma_i^{(k)}\langle j \rangle = \begin{cases} 1 - \gamma_i\langle j \rangle & \text{if } j = \frac{i}{k} \\ \gamma_i\langle j \rangle & \text{otherwise} \end{cases}$$

Claim: There exists a solution configuration F to (A, T) iff there exists a solution assignment Π to (U, Γ).

For both directions of the proof we shall use the following definitions They each stand for the computation performed by the first layer of nodes when the net is given some stimulus (of one particular type) in the task:

$$\zeta_i = Comp_F^A(0 \cdot \gamma_i)[^P_{V_1}] \quad \text{(from } T_1\text{)}$$

$$\beta_i^{(j)} = Comp_F^A(0 \cdot \gamma_i^{(j)})[^P_{V_1}] \quad \text{(from } T_2\text{)}$$

$$\eta_i = Comp_F^A(1 \cdot \gamma_i)[^P_{V_1}] \quad \text{(from } T_3\text{)}$$

proof ($\exists F \Leftarrow \exists \Pi$): Specify the node functions as follows:

$$f_{1,j}(a \cdot b) = \begin{cases} E(-d + 2da + 2db) & \text{if } \Pi\langle j \rangle = 1 \\ E(-d - 2da + 2db) & \text{if } \Pi\langle j \rangle = 0 \end{cases}$$

$$f_{2,i}(\alpha) = E(e_{2,i}(\alpha))$$

where

$$e_{2,i}(\alpha) = -d + 2d \sum_{k=1}^{|G_i|} W_{i,k} \times (\zeta_i \langle \tfrac{i}{k} \rangle - \alpha \langle k \rangle)$$

$$W_{i,k} = \begin{cases} +1 & \text{if } \gamma_i \langle \tfrac{i}{k} \rangle = 1 \\ -1 & \text{if } \gamma_i \langle \tfrac{i}{k} \rangle = 0 \end{cases}$$

The above expression for $e_{2,i}$ is not in standard form, but it is straightforward to rearrange it so that it is.

We shall check that each subtask is performed correctly by this configuration. Observe

$$f_{1,j}(0 \cdot 0) = E(-d + 0 + 0) \overset{d}{\models} 0$$

$$f_{1,j}(0 \cdot 1) = E(-d + 0 + 2d) \overset{d}{\models} 1$$

Hence $Comp_F^A(0 \cdot \alpha)[_{V_1}^P] \not\models^d \alpha$. Consequently $\zeta_i \not\models^d \gamma_i$. Also, for those functions in the second row,

$$f_{2,i}(\zeta_i[_{p(v_{2,i})}^{V_1}]) = E(-d + 2d \sum_k W_{i,k}(\zeta_i\langle \tfrac{i}{k} \rangle - \zeta_i\langle \tfrac{i}{k} \rangle)) \models^d 0$$

The agreement holds because the total value of the summation is 0. This argument applies to each value of i, and hence for high d, the first items are correctly retrieved $\mathcal{M}_F^A \supseteq T_1$.

Consider a typical item in T_2. Note that $\beta_i^{(k)} \not\models^d \gamma_i^{(k)}$, and that $\beta_i^{(k)}\langle \tfrac{i}{k} \rangle$ therefore differs from $\gamma_i\langle \tfrac{i}{k} \rangle$ as d increases. The absolute difference converges monotonically to 1, so we have

$$f_{2,i}(\beta_i^{(k)}[_{p(v_{2,i})}^{V_1}]) = E(-d + 2d \sum W_{i,k}(\zeta_i\langle \tfrac{i}{k} \rangle - \beta_i^{(k)}\langle \tfrac{i}{k} \rangle)) \models^d 1$$

Here we know the agreement for high d holds because the total value of the summation tends to 1 as d increases. Since the equation is valid for all $1 \leq k \leq |G_i|$ for each γ_i, $\mathcal{M}_F^A \supseteq T_2$ for high d.

Next we consider a typical item in T_3. For all nodes in layer 1, observe

if $\Pi\langle j \rangle = 1, \quad f_{1,j}(1 \cdot x) = E(-d + 2d + 2dx) \models^d 1$ for $x \in \{0,1\}$

if $\Pi\langle j \rangle = 0, \quad f_{1,j}(1 \cdot x) = E(-d - 2d + 2dx) \not\models^d 0$ for $x \in \{0,1\}$

Hence $f_{1,j}(1 \cdot x) \models^d \Pi\langle j \rangle$ and consequently $\eta_i \models^d \Pi$ for all i. Examining the second layer, we know

$$f_{2,i}(\eta_i[_{p(v_{2,i})}^{V_1}]) = E(-d + 2d \sum W_{i,k}(\zeta_i\langle \tfrac{i}{k} \rangle - \eta_i\langle \tfrac{i}{k} \rangle)) \models^d 1$$

because as d increases the summation converges to some integer representing the number of places where $\zeta_i[_{G_i}^U]$ is not equal to $\eta_i[_{G_i}^U]$, that is, the number of places where $\gamma_i[_{G_i}^U]$ is not equal to $\Pi[_{G_i}^U]$. By the initial assumption about Π, this integer is at least 1, so the agreement holds (for high d). This demonstrates that $\mathcal{M}_F^A \supseteq T_3$ for high d.

By selecting some value for d that satisfies all the above agreements, $\mathcal{M}_F^A \supseteq T$, and this completes the proof of one direction of the claim.

Proof ($\exists F \Rightarrow \exists \Pi$): Let $y_{j,k}$ and $z_{i,k}$ be the weights employed in the node functions as follows: for all i, j, $1 \leq i \leq m$, $1 \leq j \leq w$, let

$$f_{1,j}(a \cdot b) = E(y_{j,0} + y_{j,1}a + y_{j,2}b)$$

$$f_{2,i}(\alpha) = E(z_{i,0} + \sum_{k=1}^{|G_i|} z_{i,k}\alpha\langle k \rangle)$$

Define the satisfying assignment:

$$\Pi\langle j \rangle = \begin{cases} 1 & \text{if } y_{j,1}y_{j,2} > 0 \\ 0 & \text{otherwise} \end{cases}$$

We must show Π satisfies (U, Γ).

By assumption, the configuration F performs T_1 and T_2, so we know for each i, $1 \leq i \leq m$ and for any k, $1 \leq k \leq |G_i|$

$$f_{2,i}(\zeta_i[^{V_1}_{p(v_{2,i})}]) \models 0$$

$$f_{2,i}(\beta_i^{(k)}[^{V_1}_{p(v_{2,i})}]) \models 1$$

so

$$f_{2,i}(\zeta_i[^{V_1}_{p(v_{2,i})}]) < f_{2,i}(\beta_i^{(k)}[^{V_1}_{p(v_{2,i})}])$$

$$E(z_{i,0} + \sum_c z_{i,c}\,\zeta_i\langle\tfrac{i}{c}\rangle) < E(z_{i,0} + \sum_c z_{i,c}\,\beta_i^{(k)}\langle\tfrac{i}{c}\rangle)$$

but $\zeta_i\langle j \rangle = \beta_i^{(k)}\langle j \rangle$ for all $j \neq \tfrac{i}{k}$, or more specifically $\zeta_i\langle\tfrac{i}{c}\rangle \neq \beta_i^{(k)}\langle\tfrac{i}{c}\rangle$ only when $c = k$. Therefore

$$z_{i,k}\,\zeta_i\langle\tfrac{i}{k}\rangle < z_{i,k}\,\beta_i^{(k)}\langle\tfrac{i}{k}\rangle$$

Let $j = \tfrac{i}{k}$ and expand both sides in terms of $f_{1,j}$.

$$z_{i,k}E(y_{j,0} + y_{j,2}\,\gamma_i\langle j \rangle) < z_{i,k}E(y_{j,0} + y_{j,2}(1 - \gamma_i\langle j \rangle))$$

$$z_{i,k}\,y_{j,2}\,\gamma_i\langle\tfrac{i}{k}\rangle < z_{i,k}\,y_{j,2}\,(1 - \gamma_i\langle\tfrac{i}{k}\rangle)$$

if $\gamma_i\langle j \rangle = 0$ then $0 < z_{i,k}\,y_{j,2}$ \hfill (B.1)

if $\gamma_i\langle j \rangle = 1$ then $z_{i,k}\,y_{j,2} < 0$ \hfill (B.2)

Again, by assumption that F configures the net for T_1 and T_2,

$$f_{2,i}(\zeta_i[^{V_1}_{p(v_{2,i})}] \models 0$$

$$f_{2,i}(\eta_i[^{V_1}_{p(v_{2,i})}] \models 1$$

$$E(z_{i,0} + \sum_k z_{i,k}\, \zeta_i\langle \tfrac{i}{k} \rangle)) < E(z_{i,0} + \sum_k z_{i,k}\, \eta_i\langle \tfrac{i}{k} \rangle))$$

$$\sum_k z_{i,k}\, \zeta_i\langle \tfrac{i}{k} \rangle < \sum_k z_{i,k}\, \eta_i\langle \tfrac{i}{k} \rangle$$

For this to be true for a given i, there must be at least one k such that

$$z_{i,k}\, \zeta_i\langle \tfrac{i}{k} \rangle < z_{i,k}\, \eta_i\langle \tfrac{i}{k} \rangle$$

Letting $j = \tfrac{i}{k}$ and expanding both sides as $f_{1,j}$,

$$z_{i,k}\, E(y_{j,0} + y_{j,2}\, \gamma_i\langle j \rangle)) < z_{i,k}\, E(y_{j,0} + y_{j,1} + y_{j,2}\, \gamma_i\langle j \rangle))$$

$$0 < z_{i,k}\, y_{j,1}$$

From this and (B.1), we find that

$$\gamma_i\langle j \rangle = 0 \Rightarrow 0 < z_{i,k}\, z_{i,k}\, y_{j,1}\, y_{j,2} \Rightarrow 0 < y_{j,1}\, y_{j,2} \Rightarrow \Pi\langle j \rangle = 1$$

Similarly, $\gamma_i\langle j \rangle = 1 \Rightarrow \Pi\langle j \rangle = 0$. Summarizing, for all γ_i there exists a k such that $\gamma_i\langle \tfrac{i}{k} \rangle \neq \Pi\langle \tfrac{i}{k} \rangle$, or rather $\gamma_i[^U_{G_i}] \neq \Pi[^U_{G_i}]$. That is, Π satisfies (U, Γ) and the claim is proved. $\square$

The claim establishes that the reduction from SAT is valid. Since the transformation can be performed in polynomial time, $Perf_{LLFns}$ is NP-hard.

$Perf_{LLFns}$ is in NP if there is a polynomial-time procedure to write down values for all the weights. For the case where the weights are truly real-valued (meaning that a weight would have a potentially infinite number of digits), it has not yet been proved that there is a finite approximation that is effectively equivalent to the real numbers (as

Hong has done for LSFns). However, for the more realistic case of fixed resolution in each "real" weight, specifying the configuration is easily performed in polynomial time. With that minor caveat, we have proved $Perf_{LLFns}$ is NP-complete. □

Three aspects of LLFns are crucial to the preceding proof: E is monotonic, E is bounded, and e is linear. Other aspects were convenient but not necessary; for example, every node had a fixed E function, every node had the *same* E function, and that E was onto the unit interval $[0, 1]$. We proved the theorem for LLFns only in order to avoid excessive abstraction, but the theorem is extendible to other node function sets.

If we define the quasi-linear functions (QLFns) as all those functions of the form $E(e(\alpha))$, where e is linear and E is a bounded and monotonic, then for some appropriate definition of agreement we have

COROLLARY 25 $Perf_{QLFns}$ is NP-complete.

The theorem is probably extendible to different manifestations of nonlinearity, but we note that something about E should be nonlinear, for if E (as well as e) is linear, then the net as a whole can implement only linear mappings. From the point of view of connectionists, this is uninteresting.

Appendix C

Proof for Case Without Don't Cares

I don't care, Daddy.
—*Tilke Mary Judd*

The proof of theorem 1 uses the * symbol to denote 'don't cares' in the response strings. This is often not a feature of connectionist experiments so the following proof avoids the * in order to demonstrate that it is not an important change to the model.

THEOREM 26 *Perf*$_{AOFns}$ *is NP-complete even when responses have no "don't-cares."*

Proof: by reduction from 3SAT. The proof is modeled on the one for theorem 1. Let the 3SAT problem be (Z, C) where Z is a set of variables $\{\zeta_1, \zeta_2, \zeta_3, \ldots\}$ and C is a set of disjunctive clauses over them. Let $w = |Z|$ be the number of variables and $m = |C|$ the number of clauses. For (Z, C) to be satisfiable, there must be an assignment $\Pi : Z \to \{0, 1\}$ such that at least one literal in each clause has value 1.

Formally, the 3SAT instance (Z, C) is reduced to (A, T), where

$$A = (P, V, S, R, E)$$
$$S = \{a, b, d, e\}$$
$$V = \{u_i, v_i, w_i, x_i, y_i, z_i : \zeta_i \in Z\} \cup \{c_j : C_j \in C\}$$

$$R = \{u_i, x_i, y_i, v_i : \zeta_i \in Z\} \cup \{c_j : C_j \in C\}$$
$$P = S \cup V$$
$$E = \{(a, w_i), (a, z_i), (b, w_i), (b, z_i),$$
$$(w_i, u_i), (w_i, x_i), (w_i, y_i), (z_i, x_i), (z_i, y_i), (z_i, v_i),$$
$$(d, u_i), (d, v_i), : \zeta_i \in Z\}$$
$$\cup \{(w_i, c_j) : \zeta_i \in C_j\} \cup \{(z_i, c_j) : \overline{\zeta_i} \in C_j\} \cup \{(e, c_j) : C_j \in C\}$$
$$T = \{I_1, I_2, I_3\}$$
$$I_1 = (0\,0\,1\,1, (0\,0\,0\,0)^w\,0^m)$$
$$I_2 = (1\,1\,1\,0, (1\,1\,1\,1)^w\,0^m)$$
$$I_3 = (0\,1\,0\,1, (0\,0\,1\,0)^w\,1^m)$$

This construction is explained in a two-stage example. Stage 1: For every variable $\zeta_j \in Z$ construct the partial architecture and partial task shown in figure C.1. This is very similar to figure 4.1 on page 45. The differences are that w and z are no longer network outputs; instead they go to new nodes u and v, which are network outputs. Also there is a new input, d, which goes only to these new nodes. In the task, note that all response bits for u and v are the same as they were for w and z except that the *'s have been replaced by 0's (arbitrarily). In the items where w and z had been defined, d is a 1; in the items where w and z had been 'don't cares', d is a 0.

From items 1 and 2 we know

$$f_u(f_w(0,0), 1) = 0 \neq 1 = f_u(f_w(1,1), 1). \tag{C.1}$$

Hence

$$f_w(0,0) \neq f_w(1,1). \tag{C.2}$$

Similarly

$$f_z(0,0) \neq f_z(1,1). \tag{C.3}$$

By comparing item 2 and item 3, we know

$$f_x(f_w(1,1), f_z(1,1)) = 1 \neq 0 = f_x(f_w(0,1), f_z(0,1))$$

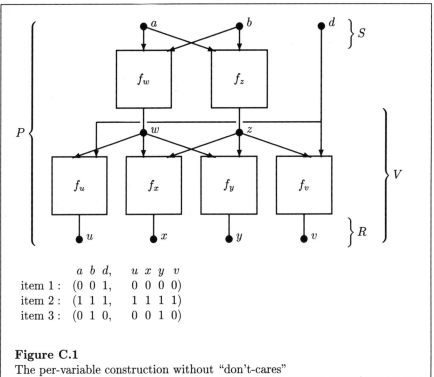

	a	b	$d,$	u	x	y	v
item 1 :	(0	0	1,	0	0	0	0)
item 2 :	(1	1	1,	1	1	1	1)
item 3 :	(0	1	0,	0	0	1	0)

Figure C.1
The per-variable construction without "don't-cares"

$f_w(1, 1) \neq f_w(0, 1)$ or $f_z(1, 1) \neq f_z(0, 1)$,

and by using (C.2) and (C.3)

$$f_w(0, 0) = f_w(0, 1) \text{ or } f_z(0, 0) = f_z(0, 1). \tag{C.4}$$

By comparing item 1 and item 3 we know

$$f_y(f_w(0, 0), f_z(0, 0)) = 0 \neq 1 = f_y(f_w(0, 1), f_z(0, 1))$$

$$f_w(0, 0) \neq f_w(0, 1) \text{ or } f_z(0, 0) \neq f_z(0, 1) \tag{C.5}$$

We will associate some SAT variable ζ_j with the group of nodes in this construction. For mnemonic value and brevity, let $\langle \zeta \rangle$ stand for the truth of the inequality $f_w(0, 0) \neq f_w(0, 1)$. And let $\langle \bar{\zeta} \rangle$ stand for the truth of the inequality $f_z(0,0) \neq f_z(0,1)$. Translating (C.4) and (C.5) we have

$$(\text{not}\langle \zeta \rangle \text{ or } \text{not}\langle \overline{\zeta} \rangle) \text{ and } (\langle \zeta \rangle \text{ or } \langle \overline{\zeta} \rangle)$$

which implies $\langle \zeta \rangle = \text{not}\langle \overline{\zeta} \rangle$.

Stage 2: For each clause in the SAT system construct a single node in the second layer of the architecture with inputs from all nodes associated with its participating literals and an input from post e. Putting variables' nodes and the clause node together, we get what is shown in figure C.2. It shows the construction for an example SAT system consisting of only one clause $(\zeta_1, \overline{\zeta_2}, \overline{\zeta_3})$. Observe that each item consists of the stimulus from an item from figure C.1, a new stimulus bit for e, three replications of the associated response (one per variable), and another response bit for the clause node.

Claim: The constructed architecture can perform the task iff the SAT instance is satisfiable.

Proof: By inspecting item 1 and item 3,

$$f_c(f_w^1(0,0), f_z^2(0,0), f_z^3(0,0), 1) = 0$$

$$f_c(f_w^1(0,1), f_z^2(0,1), f_z^3(0,1), 1) = 1$$

Since not all of the arguments can be the same, conclude

$$\langle \zeta_1 \rangle \text{ or } \langle \overline{\zeta_2} \rangle \text{ or } \langle \overline{\zeta_3} \rangle.$$

Now if Π exists then let $\langle \zeta_j \rangle = \Pi(\zeta_j)$, that is, let $f_w^j(0,0) = 0$ and $f_w^j(0,1) = \Pi(\zeta_j)$ and $f_w^j(1,1) = 1$ for all j, or more definitively, let

$$f_w^j = \begin{cases} \text{OR} & \text{if } \Pi(\zeta_j) = 1 \\ \text{AND} & \text{if } \Pi(\zeta_j) = 0 \end{cases} \quad \text{and} \quad f_z^j = \begin{cases} \text{AND} & \text{if } \Pi(\zeta_j) = 1 \\ \text{OR} & \text{if } \Pi(\zeta_j) = 0 \end{cases}.$$

For all variables ζ_j let $f_u^j = f_v^j = f_x^j = \text{AND}$ and $f_y^j = \text{OR}$, and for the clause node let $f_c = \text{OR}$. The items are all performed correctly.

Conversely, if a configuration exists let $\Pi(\zeta_j) = \langle \zeta_j \rangle = f_w^j(0,1) \oplus f_w^j(0,0)$, and observe $\langle \zeta_1 \rangle$ or $\langle \overline{\zeta_2} \rangle$ or $\langle \overline{\zeta_3} \rangle$ implies $\zeta_1 = 1$ or $\overline{\zeta_2} = 1$ or $\overline{\zeta_3} = 1$ as required. This proves the claim.   □

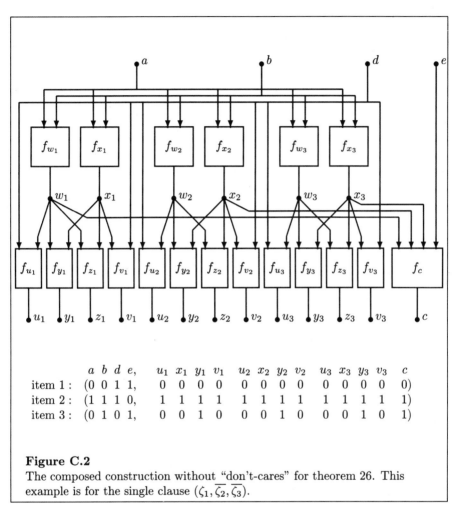

Figure C.2
The composed construction without "don't-cares" for theorem 26. This
example is for the single clause $(\zeta_1, \overline{\zeta_2}, \overline{\zeta_3})$.

The extension to multiclause systems involves an extra second-level
node for each new clause. It should be clear.

Thus we have SAT $\propto Perf_{AOFns}$ and it is easy to see that the algorithm for the transformation runs in polynomial time.

Finally, as argued for theorem 1, $Perf_{SAFns} \in NP$. Hence $Perf_{SAFns}$
is NP-complete. $\qquad\qquad\qquad\qquad\qquad\qquad\qquad\qquad\qquad\qquad\quad$ $\square$

Recall that items 1 and 2 produced equation C.1 which forced a relationship between $f_w(0,0)$ and $f_w(1,1)$ given by equation C.2. From items 2 and 3 we know

$$f_u(f_w(1,1),1) = 1 \neq 0 = f_u(f_w(0,1),0),$$

but this does not force any particular relationship between $f_w(1,1)$ and $f_w(0,1)$ (nor do items 1 and 3 force any relationship between $f_w(0,0)$ and $f_w(0,1)$). Hence $f_w(0,1)$ might just as well have been specified as a 'don't-care' as it was in the proof for theorem 1. Thus input d and node u have been employed here as a switch to simulate the do-care/don't-care distinction for the output from node w. Similarly, d and v have been used for z. A similar technique using input e simulated the do-care/don't-care distinction for the output from node c.

I believe these techniques could be applied generally. They make this theorem stronger at the expense of extra complications in the proof. I prefer to make use of the * in the other theorems in order to simplify their proofs.

Appendix D

Proof for Planar Case with LSFns

A good proof is one that makes us wiser.
— *Yuri Manin*

The proof for theorem 16 used LUFns as its node function set and hence does not cover the specific (and conventional) case of node function sets that are linearly separable. This appendix gives a proof that is strong enough to cover LSFns. In particular, it gives a construction for a crossover using SAFns, which is a node function set described in appendix A. Because SAFns $\subseteq$ LSFns $\subseteq$ LUFns, this theorem is sufficient to cover the linearly separable case whereas the proof for theorem 16 was not.

In fact, theorem 16 could have been proved by simply reducing from planar 3SAT (which is proved *NP*-complete by the following construction), but for those readers who are not familiar with the intuition behind that result, it would be a non-illuminating proof.

Figure D.1 is the construction used in [Lic82, fig. 4] as a crossover box in his proof of *NP*-completeness for planar SAT. For that purpose the circles were interpreted as variables and the squares as clauses. The diagram is a demonstration that the following SAT system has a planar layout:

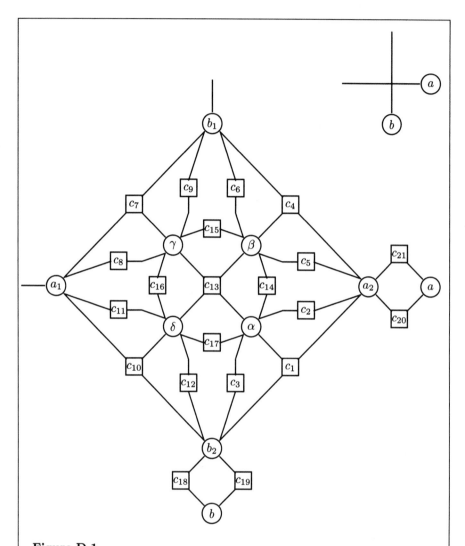

Figure D.1
Construction from Lichtenstein for Planar SAT. The prototypical
crossover of two lines shown in the upper right is replaced by the much
larger construction, which provides the same constraints as the smaller
one would have.

clauses 1–3:	$(\overline{a_2} \vee \overline{b_2} \vee \alpha)(a_2 \vee \overline{\alpha})(b_2 \vee \overline{\alpha})$	i.e. $a_2 b_2 \Leftrightarrow \alpha$;
clauses 4–6:	$(\overline{a_2} \vee b_1 \vee \beta)(a_2 \vee \overline{\beta})(\overline{b_1} \vee \beta)$	i.e. $a_2\overline{b_1} \Leftrightarrow \beta$;
clauses 7–9:	$(a_1 \vee b_1 \vee \gamma)(\overline{a_1} \vee \overline{\gamma})(\overline{b_1} \vee \overline{\gamma})$	i.e. $\overline{a_1}\overline{b_1} \Leftrightarrow \gamma$;
clauses 10–12:	$(a_1 \vee \overline{b_2} \vee \delta)(\overline{a_1} \vee \overline{\delta})(b_2 \vee \overline{\delta})$	i.e. $\overline{a_1}b_2 \Leftrightarrow \delta$;
clause 13:	$(\alpha \vee \beta \vee \gamma \vee \delta)$	
clauses 14–17:	$(\overline{\alpha} \vee \overline{\beta})(\overline{\beta} \vee \overline{\gamma})(\overline{\gamma} \vee \overline{\delta})(\overline{\delta} \vee \overline{\alpha})$	
clauses 18–19:	$(\overline{a} \vee a_2)(a \vee \overline{a_2})$	i.e. $a \Leftrightarrow a_2$;
clauses 20–21:	$(\overline{b} \vee b_2)(b \vee \overline{b_2})$	i.e. $b \Leftrightarrow b_2$;

This construction is used in the proof of the following theorem:

THEOREM 27 For any node function set that includes SAFns, loading is NP-complete even for 2-layered architectures with planar SCI graphs.

Proof: I give only a construction for a "crossover box" that can be used to eliminate one crossing of connections as they might occur in the proof of theorem 15.

For this purpose figure D.1 is reinterpreted as the plan view of an architecture, the circles being first-layer nodes and the squares being second-layer nodes. To accompany this architecture, a task is constructed to mimic the effect of each clause. Let us use the techniques of constructing items that are used in the proof of theorem 23. First, two items ensure that $f_v(0,0) = 0$ and $f_v(1,1) = 1$ for all variables $v \in \{a, a_1, a_2, b, b_1, b_2, \alpha, \beta, \gamma, \delta\}$:

```
a a₁ a₂ b b₁ b₂ α β γ δ        a a₁ a₂ b b₁ b₂ α β γ δ c₁ c₂ c₃ ... c₂₁
00 00 00 00 00 00 00 00 00 00  ↦  0 0  0 0 0  0 0 0 0 0 * * *    *
11 11 11 11 11 11 11 11 11 11  ↦  1 1  1 1 1  1 1 1 1 1 * * *    *
```

Second, for each of Lichtenstein's clauses two items are produced as in the following example:

```
a a₁ a₂ b b₁ b₂ α β γ δ        a a₁ a₂ b b₁ b₂ α β γ δ c₁ c₂ c₃ ... c₂₁
** ** 11 ** ** 11 00 ** ** **  ↦  * * * * * * * * * * 0 * *    *
** ** 01 ** ** 01 01 ** ** **  ↦  * * * * * * * * * * 1 * *    *
```

This corresponds to $(\overline{a_2} \vee \overline{b_2} \vee \alpha)$, which is clause 1. These two items ensure that

$$f_{c_1}(f_{a_2}(1,1), f_{b_2}(1,1), f_\alpha(0,0)) = 0 \neq 1 = f_{c_1}(f_{a_2}(0,1), f_{b_2}(0,1), f_\alpha(0,1))$$

The L.H.S. equals $f_{c_1}(1,1,0)$ and because it must be unequal to the R.H.S., i.e. $f_{c_1}(f_{a_2}(0,1), f_{b_2}(0,1), f_\alpha(0,1))$, at least one of the arguments must be different:

$$f_{a_2}(0,1) \neq 1 \quad \text{or} \quad f_{b_2}(0,1) \neq 1 \quad \text{or} \quad f_\alpha(0,1) \neq 0$$

Harking back to earlier proofs, it is the values of these functions on inputs $(0,1)$ that are the focal indeterminants of the system. The direct correspondence to $(\overline{a_2} \vee \overline{b_2} \vee \alpha)$ should be clear.   □

Appendix E

The $O()$ and $\Omega()$ Notation

The $O()$ notation (pronounced "big Oh of" or "order") is a convenient way of stating an asymptotic relationship between two functions. Technically, to say $f = O(g)$ means that the function $f(n)$ can be bounded by some linear function of the function $g(n)$:

$$f = O(g) \iff \exists d,\ c > 0\ \ \forall n f(n) \leq cg(n) + d.$$

The function f is typically the scale-up function that is being discussed (and it is often unnamed). The argument, n, is usually an obvious metric on the size of the problem at hand. The layman can interpret "the running time is $O(n^2)$" as "the running time scales up no worse than n^2."

The $\Omega()$ notation is pronounced "big omega." Whereas the $O()$ talks about an upper bound on a function, $\Omega()$ talks about a lower bound. Its technical definition is the same as $O()$ except for the direction of the inequality:

$$f = \Omega(g) \iff \exists d,\ c > 0\ \ \forall n f(n) \geq cg(n) + d.$$

The layman can interpret "the running time is $\Omega(n^4)$" as "the running time scales up at least as badly as n^4."

Bibliography

[ACP87]   Arnborg, S., D. G. Corneil, and A. Proskurowski. Complexity of finding embeddings in a k-tree. *SIAM J. Algebraic and Discrete Methods*, 8(2), April 1987.

[AHS85]   Ackley, D. H., G. E. Hinton, and T. J. Sejnowski. A learning algorithm for Boltzmann machines. *Cognitive Science*, 9:147–169, 1985.

[AHU74]   Aho, Alfred V., John E. Hopcroft, and Jeffrey D. Ullman. *The design and analysis of computer algorithms*. Addison-Wesley, 1974.

[Ale84]   Aleksander, Igor. *Artificial Vision for Robots*. Chapman & Hall, New York, 1984.

[And72]   Anderson, James A. A simple neural network generating an interactive memory. *Mathematical Biosciences*, 14:197–220, 1972.

[AP88]   Arnborg, Stefan, and Andrzej Proskurowski. Linear time algorithms for NP-hard problems restricted to partial k-trees. *Discrete Applied Mathematics*, 1988. To appear.

[AR88]   Anderson, James A. and Edward Rosenfeld, editors. *Neurocomputing— Foundations of Research*. MIT Press, Cambridge, Massachusetts, 1988.

[AS83]   Angluin, D., and C. Smith. Inductive inference: theory and methods. *Computing Surveys*, 15(3):237–269, September 1983.

[BA85]   Barto, A. G., and P. Anandan. Pattern recognizing stochastic learning automata. *IEEE Transactions on Systems, Man, and Cybernetics*, 15:360–375, 1985.

[Bac42]   Bacon, R. *Opus maius*. Pressus Gutenbergus, 1442. Manuscript received 1274.

[Bar82]   Barahona, Fransisco. On the computational complexity of Ising spin glass models. *Journal of Physics A: Math. Gen.*, 15:3241–3253, 1982.

[Bar85]   Barto, Andrew G. Learning by statistical cooperation of self-interested neuron-like computing elements. *Human Neurobiology*, 4:229–256, 1985.

[BB75]   Blum, L., and M. Blum. Toward a mathematical theory of inductive inference. *Information and Control*, 28:125–155, 1975.

[BEHW87]   Blumer, Anselm, Andrzej Ehrenfeucht, David Haussler, and Manfred K. Warmuth. Occam's razor. *Information Processing Letters*, 24:377–380, 1987.

[BR88]   Blum, Avrim, and Ronald L. Rivest. Training a 3-node neural net
           is *NP*-complete. In David S. Touretzky, editor, *Advances in Neural
           Information Processing Systems I*, pages 494–501, Morgan Kaufmann,
           San Mateo, California, 1989.

[BV87]   Baldi, Pierre, and Santosh S. Venkatesh. On properties of networks of
           neuron-like elements. In Dana Z. Anderson, editor, *Neural Information
           Processing Systems ('87)*, pages 41–51, American Institute of Physics,
           New York, 1988.

[Car50]   Carnap, R. *Logical Foundations of Probability*. University of Chicago
           Press, Chicago, Illinois, 1950.

[CES81]   Chung, M. J., W. M. Evangelist, and I. H. Sudborough. Some addi-
           tional examples of bandwidth constrained *NP*-complete problems. In
           Proceedings of 1981 Conference on Information Science and Systems,
           Dept. of E.E., Johns Hopkins University, 1981.

[Cho80]   Chomsky, N. Initial states and steady states. In M. Piatelli-Palmarini,
           editor, *Language and Learning*, pages 107–130, Harvard University
           Press, Cambridge, Massachusetts, 1980.

[CK87]   Corneil, D. G., and J. M. Keil. A dynamic programming approach to
           the dominating set problem on *k*-trees. *SIAM J. Algebraic and Discrete
           Methods*, 8(4), October 1987.

[DH73]   Duda, Richard O., and Peter E. Hart. *Pattern Classification and Scene
           Analysis*. Wiley, New York, 1973.

[DM81]   Dieterich, T.G., and R.S. Michalski. Inductive learning of structural
           descriptions: Evaluation criteria and comparative review of selected
           methods. *Artificial Intelligence*, 16:601–617, 1981.

[GGJK78]   Garey, M. R., R. L. Graham, D. S. Johnson, and D. E. Knuth. Com-
           plexity results for bandwidth minimization. *SIAM Journal of Applied
           Mathematics*, 34(3):477–495, 1978.

[GJ79]   Garey, M. R., and D. S. Johnson. *Computers and Intractability: A
           Guide to the Theory of NP-Completeness*. W. H. Freeman, San Fran-
           cisco, California, 1979.

[God87]   Godbeer, Gail H. *The Computational Complexity of the Stable Con-
           figuration Problem for Connectionist Models*. Master's thesis, Dept.
           Computer Science, University of Toronto, September 1987.

[Gol67]   Gold, E. Language identification in the limit. *Information and Control*,
           10:447–474, 1967.

[Hin87]   Hinton, Geoffrey E. *Connectionist Learning Procedures.* Technical Report CMU-CS-87-115, Computer Science Department, Carnegie-Mellon University, Pittsburgh, Pennsylvania 15213, 1987.

[HMS66]   Hunt, E. B., J. Marin, and P.J. Stone. *Experiments in Induction.* Academic Press, New York, 1966.

[Hon87]   Hong, Jai-wei. *On Connectionist Models.* Technical Report, Dept. Computer Science, University of Chicago, Chicago, Illinois, May 1987.

[Hop82]   Hopfield, J. J. Neural networks and physical systems with emergent collective computational capabilities. In *Proceedings of the National Academy of Sciences*, pages 2554–2558, 1982.

[HS86]   Hinton, Geoffrey E., and Terrence J. Sejnowski. Learning and relearning in Boltzmann machines. In David E. Rumelhart and Jay L. McClelland, editors, *Parallel Distributed Processing: Explorations in the Microstructure of Cognition, vol.1: Foundations*, chapter 7, MIT Press, Cambridge, Massachusetts, 1986.

[HV86]   Hampson, S. E., and D. J. Volper. Linear function neurons: Structure and training. *Biological Cybernetics*, 53:203–217, 1986.

[HV87]   Hampson, S. E., and D. J. Volper. Disjunctive models of boolean category representation. *Biological Cybernetics*, 56:121–137, 1987.

[HW79]   Hubel, David H., and Torsten N. Weisel. Brain mechanisms of vision. In *The Brain*, chapter VII, Freeman, 1979. Also appeared in September 1979 issue of Scientific American.

[Jud87a]   Judd, J. S. *Complexity of Connectionist Learning with Various Node Functions.* Technical Report 87-60, University of Massachusetts, Amherst, Massachusetts, 1987.

[Jud87b]   Judd, J. S. Learning in networks is hard. In *Proceedings of the First International Conference on Neural Networks*, pages 685–692, I.E.E.E., San Diego, California, June 1987.

[Jud88a]   Judd, J. S. *A Generalization of Bandwidth.* Technical Report, California Institute of Technology, Pasadena, California 91125, 1989. In preparation. Still.

[Jud88b]   Judd, J. S. The intractability of learning in connectionist networks. 1988. Submitted for publication.

[Jud88c]   Judd, J. S. On the complexity of loading shallow neural networks. *Journal of Complexity*, September 1988. Special issue on Neural Computation.

[KLPV87]   Kearns, M., Ming Li, Leonard Pitt, and Leslie Valiant. On the learn-
           ability of boolean formulae. In *Proc. 19th Symposium on Theory of
           Computing*, pages 285–295, ACM, New York, 1987.

[Koh77]   Kohonen, T. *Associative Memory—A System Theoretic Approach*.
           Springer-Verlag, Berlin, 1977.

[Koh84]   Kohonen, T. *Self Organization and Associative Memory*. Springer-
           Verlag, Berlin, 1984.

[lC85]   le Cun, Yann. Une procedure d'apprentissage pour reseau a sequil
           assymetrique. *Proceedings of Cognitiva*, 85:599–604, 1985.

[Lic82]   Lichtenstein, David. Planar formulae and their uses. *SIAM Journal of
           Computing*, 11(2):329–343, 1982.

[Lip87]   Lipscomb, John. *On the Computational Complexity of Finding a Con-
           nectionist Model's Stable State Vector*. Master's thesis, Dept. Computer
           Science, University of Toronto, October 1987.

[Lit87]   Littlestone, Nick. Learning quickly when irrelevant attributes abound:
           A new linear-threshold algorithm. In *28th Symposium on Foundations
           of Computer Science*, pages 68–77, I.E.E.E., 1987.

[Mit77]   Mitchell, T. M. Version spaces: a candidate elimination approach to
           rule learning. In *Proceedings of IJCAI 5*, pages 305–310, 1977.

[MP72]   Minsky, Marvin, and Seymour Papert. *Perceptrons: An Introduction
           to Computational Geometry*. MIT Press, Cambridge, Massachusetts,
           1972.

[MR86]   McClelland, Jay L., and David E. Rumelhart, editors. *Parallel Dis-
           tributed Processing: Explorations in the Microstructure of Cognition,
           vol.2: Psychological and Biological Models*. MIT Press, Cambridge,
           MA., 1986.

[MS81]   Monien, Burkhard, and Ivan Hal Sudborough. Bandwidth constrained
           NP-complete problems. In *13th Symposium on Theory of Computing*,
           pages 207–217, 1981.

[Mur65]   Muroga, S. Lower bounds of the number of threshold functions and a
           maximum weight. *Transactions on Electronic Computers*, 14:136–148,
           1965.

[Mur71]   Muroga, S. *Threshold Logic and its Applications*. Wiley-Interscience,
           1971.

[Nil65]   Nilsson, Nils J. *Learning Machines: Foundations of Trainable Pattern-Classification Machines.* McGraw-Hill, 1965.

[NL77]   Narendra, Kumpati S., and S. Lakshmivarahan. Learning automata—a critique. *Journal of Cybernetics and Information Science,* 1, fall 1977.

[NT74]   Narendra, Kumpati S., and M. A. L. Thathatchar. Learning automata—a survey. *I.E.E.E. Trans on Systems, Man, and Cybernetics,* SMC-4(4):323–334, July 1974.

[Omo87]   Omohundro, Stephen M. *Efficient Algorithms with Neural Network Behaviour.* Technical Report UIUCDCS-R-87-1331, Dept. Computer Science, University of Illinois at Urbana-Champaign, 1304 W. Springfield Ave., Urbana, Illinois 61801, April 1987.

[OSW86]   Osherson, Daniel N, Michael Stob, and Scott Weinstein. *Systems that Learn.* MIT Press, Cambridge, Massachusetts, 1986.

[Par85]   Parker, D. B. *Learning Logic.* Technical Report TR-47, Massachusetts Institute of Technology, Cambridge, Massachusetts 02195, 1985.

[Por87]   Porat, Sara. *Stability and Looping in Connectionist Models with Asymmetric Weights.* Technical Report TR 210, Computer Science Dept., University of Rochester, Rochester, New York 14627, March 1987.

[PS85]   Peled, Uri N., and Bruno Simeone. Poynomial-time algorithms for regular set-covering and threshold synthesis. *Discrete Applied Mathematics,* 12:57–69, 1985.

[PV86]   Pitt, L., and L. G. Valiant. *Computational Limitations on Learning From Examples.* Technical Report TR-05-86, Aiken Computing Lab, Harvard University, 1986. To appear in JACM.

[RHM86]   Rumelhart, D. E., G. E. Hinton, and J. L. McClelland. A general framework for parallel distributed processing. In David E. Rumelhart and Jay L. McClelland, editors, *Parallel Distributed Processing: Explorations in the Microstructure of Cognition, vol.1: Foundations,* chapter 2, MIT Press, Cambridge, Massachusetts, 1986.

[RHW86]   Rumelhart, David E., Geoffrey E. Hinton, and Ronald J. Williams. Learning internal representations by error propagation. In David E. Rumelhart and Jay L. McClelland, editors, *Parallel Distributed Processing: Explorations in the Microstructure of Cognition, vol.1: Foundations,* MIT Press, Cambridge, Massachusetts, 1986.

[RM86]   Rumelhart, David E., and Jay L. McClelland, editors. *Parallel Distributed Processing: Explorations in the Microstructure of Cognition, vol.1: Foundations*. MIT Press, Cambridge, Massachusetts, 1986.

[Ros61]   Rosenblatt, Frank. *Principles of Neurodynamics: Perceptrons and the Theory of Brain Mechanisms*. Spartan Books, 6411 Chillum Place N.W., Washington, D.C., 1961.

[RS86]   Robertson, Neil, and P. D. Seymour. Graph minors. II. Algorithmic aspects of tree-width. *Journal of Algorithms*, 7:309–322, 1986.

[RZ85]   Rumelhart, D. E., and D. Zipser. Feature discovery by competitive learning. *Cognitive Science*, 9:75–112, 1985.

[Sha81]   Shapiro, Ehud Y. *Inductive Inference of Theories From Facts*. Technical Report Research Report 192, Yale University, department of Computer Science, New Haven, Connecticut, February 1981.

[SW81]   Sklansky, Jack, and Gustav N. Wassel. *Pattern Classification and Trainable Machines*. Springer-Verlag, 1981.

[TDC86]   Toulouse, Gèrard, Stanislas Dehaene, and Jean-Pierre Changeux. Spin glass model of learning by selection. *Proc. National Academy of Science USA*, 1695–1698, March 1986. Biophysics.

[Tes87]   Tesauro, Gerald. Scaling relationships in back-propogation learning: Dependence on training set size. *Complex Systems*, 1:367–372, 1987.

[TJ88]   Tesauro, Gerald, and Robert Janssens. Scaling relationships in back-propogation learning: Dependence on predicate order. *Complex Systems*, 2:39–44, 1988.

[TR81]   Thathachar, M. A. L., and K. R. Ramakrishnan. An automaton model of a hierarchical learning system. In *Proceedings of 8th Biannual Congress, Kyoto Japan*, pages 1065–1070, Control Science and Technology, 1981.

[Val84]   Valiant, L. G. A theory of the learnable. *Communications of the ACM*, 27(11):1134–1142, November 1984.

[Val85]   Valiant, L. G. Learning disjunctions of conjunctions. In *Proceedings of the 9th IJCAI*, pages 560–566, Los Angeles, California, August 1985.

[VH86]   Volper, D. J., and S. E. Hampson. Connectionist models of boolean category representation. *Biological Cybernetics*, 54:393–406, 1986.

[WC80]   Wexler, Kenneth, and Peter W. Culicover. *Formal Principles of Language Acquisition*. MIT Press, Cambridge, Massachusetts, 1980.

[WH60]   Widrow, Bernard, and Marcian E. Hoff. Adaptive switching circuits.
           In *1960 IRE WESCON Convention Record*, pages 96–104, IRE, New
           York, 1960.

[WHL85]   Wimer, T. V., S. T. Hedetniemi, and R. Laskar. A methodology for
           constructing linear graph algorithms. In *Congressium Numerantium*,
           pages 43–60, 1985.

[Wil86a]   Williams, Ronald J. The logic of activation functions. In David E.
           Rumelhart and Jay L. McClelland, editors, *Parallel Distributed Pro-
           cessing: Explorations in the Microstructure of Cognition, vol.1: Foun-
           dations*, MIT Press, Cambridge, Massachusetts, 1986.

Index